VALUE
PROPOSITIONS
THAT SELL

VALUE
PROPOSITIONS
THAT SELL

TURNING
YOUR MESSAGE
INTO A MAGNET THAT
ATTRACTS BUYERS

LISA D. DENNIS

To my mother, Marie Maillet,
who taught me all about the magic of creativity and hard work.

To Charles E. Dennis, without whom I could not have started
and grown my business, Knowledgence Associates.

And to my two mentors:
Ralph A. Goldwasser and
Peter B. Johnson

Thank you for believing in me early,
pushing me often,
and teaching me much.

CONTENTS

FOREWORD

Without a strong value proposition, it's tough to sell. Salespeople struggle to pique a prospect's interest. Quality opportunities fail to turn into closed deals. Exciting new products and services fall flat.

Yet when a company or salesperson clearly articulates the right value proposition to the right buyer, everything is different. Doors open. Momentum builds quickly. Change happens fast. And everyone is happy. In short, nailing your value proposition is essential for sales success.

That's why, for the past few years, I've been pushing Lisa Dennis to write this book. She knows more about value propositions than anyone else. Her concept of a value proposition is a whole lot more than an elevator speech, a unique selling proposition or even the one or two-line statement of value from a seller to a buyer.

She's created a methodology to help a company develop and use its value proposition that's unmatched in the profession. It starts with a Value Proposition Platform that includes identification of market sectors, target buyers and influencers, and their key business issues. When completed, Sales and Marketing have everything they need to create highly relevant, value-based messaging for use in both their content and conversations with buyers.

The Value Proposition section includes statements of the Customer Objective, the Company Offer, and the company's Differentiator. Finally, there is a section that lists Value Drivers with Quantification and Proof for each driver.

Three key points about *Value Propositions That Sell* make it unique.

- It is based on primary research conducted with B2B buyers. Each chapter starts with data from Lisa's research and expands on how your value proposition needs to reflect how buyers think and yes, how they buy and how they behave through every stage of their "buyers' journey." You'll also find supplementary research from ITSMA and The Buyer Persona Institute, insuring you the most up-to-date information available.

- The book includes two extended case studies of how Lisa guided two very different companies through the process of developing their value proposition platforms. These illustrations make the explanation come alive, as if you could sit in on the discussion of how the team chose one phrase over another, or even one keyword over another, in considering the buyers' perspective.

- It's written in the voice of a real pro, whose wisdom, experience and business sense echo in every page—direct, practical, no bull. Lisa has taken a host of companies on the value proposition journey over the past twenty years and has the battle scars to prove it. She's one of the rare practitioners who has equal credentials and commands equal respect in both camps. She speaks both languages like a native, which makes her book exceptionally useful in the real world where marketing and sales need a shared value proposition for buyers!

That's why I'm endorsing *Value Propositions That Sell* and recommending it to B2B sales and marketing leaders in companies of all sizes, to small business owners, and to sellers who need their management team to step up to developing this kind of Value Proposition Platform in their company.

Strong value propositions lead to more closed deals, shorter sales cycles, and increased revenue. Plus, everyone is more successful—including your customer.

Lisa is the Queen of the Value Proposition. Make the most of this opportunity to learn from her. It will be worth it.

Jill Konrath, Bestselling Author
Selling to Big Companies
SNAP Selling
Agile Selling
More Sales, Less Time

PREFACE

I have worked with business-to-business companies across a broad range of industries – hardware, software, healthcare, insurance, manufacturing, professional services, and others. I have been privileged to collaborate, ideate, design, build, and execute marketing and sales strategies and tactics, as well as to develop training for both marketing and sales teams. The challenge of aligning both groups to deliver a consistent, clear, and differentiated experience to buyers is still a constant struggle, even as more software tools, new methodologies, and new categories of marketing and sales techniques have evolved over the years.

The interactions between B2B buyers and sellers have become increasingly complex as buyer behavior has shifted. The very nature of marketing and selling as a discipline continues to evolve. But one thing remains unchanged – the need to uncover, define and communicate differentiated value that resonates with our target buyers.

Value Propositions –
Why They Still Matter in the Era of Buyer Control

The advent of the 'hidden sales cycle' (the stages of the buying process that buyers are conducting on their own, without sales people) has made the value of the standard value proposition formula become less and less effective. Buyers are engaging with sales later and later in the process, getting to a short list of vendors before ever speaking to any one of them. The pithy one sentence value proposition that is product or service focused does not work as well in that environment.

Given that the buyers have pretty much appropriated the sales process, it makes one wonder if we even need value props anymore. It calls into question the very "value" of a value proposition.

Should we be focusing instead on delivering "disruptors" or "insights" to a prospect, as some of the current sales methodologies advise?

My career experience (in Product Management, Marketing, and Sales roles prior to founding Knowledgence Associates in 1997) has taught me, from an inside and an outside perspective, that we need *both*, and that they should be integrated to make it easier for marketing and sales professionals to message consistently. To serve up a value proposition the right way goes beyond just delivering a "pitch" or a short statement. It must be delivered in a buyer-centric manner.

Over the past two decades, I have had the privilege of working with a host of clients of all shapes and sizes to develop their own value proposition "playbooks." These messaging platforms feed the content needs of both Marketers and Sellers, and more importantly, deliver value-based messages and conversations to drive buyer engagement. The marketing and selling game has changed exponentially and the value proposition development process needs to move with it.

The Quest for the Right Message that Sells

This book provides a direction, an approach, and a toolkit to better enable Marketing and Sales to create the right buyer conversations, via the development of a **Value Proposition Platform**™. It is designed to deliver a roadmap for messaging across all your communication channels: digital, face-to-face, and social.

Along the way, I will share some research that my company, **Knowledgence Associates®**, conducted in partnership with **IDG Connect**, to understand how value propositions fit into the decision process of buying teams making technology investment decisions. Most survey respondents were involved in all three decision focus areas: business, technical, and financial impact.

The survey results have implications that go well beyond just technology buying decisions. They speak directly to issues, challenges and needs of a broad range of B2B buyers who are focused on identifying those vendors who deliver real value that address buyer needs. There is a complete description of the research study, the partners, and the respondent demographics, along with the questions and responses, in Chapter 11. Throughout the book, I will share research, as well as analysis and insights fueled by my personal experience with customers and prospects to underscore important concepts.

Translate, then Communicate

Rather than simply delivering a description of the value a company brings to the buyer, we need to communicate the **value the buyer seeks** in achieving their goals or solving their challenge and do so in their language.

To engage the buyer in the hidden sales cycle, we must increasingly rely upon effective content marketing because that's where the sales process begins, without the sellers. This must result in an evolved value proposition creation process that fully feeds all the content needs which, in effect, are part of the sales process today.

Think that your organization doesn't have this challenge? If you asked ten different people in your organization what the value proposition is for the company and its core offering, you might be surprised to discover a lot of different answers. Getting everyone on the same page about the most important message that the company must deliver to its buyers is not automatic. So, go ahead, I challenge you to ask a handful of the staff! What you will find underscores one of the biggest challenges that most sales and marketing departments have: getting a clear and consistent message out to prospects and customers. If it isn't clear internally, you can be sure that it isn't clear among your prospects or in your markets.

With today's sophisticated and well-informed buyers, the "standard" value proposition just doesn't cut it anymore. Coupled with the increasing level of competition we all face, that makes communicating the uniqueness of your offer, and what truly differentiates you from all the other alternatives, extremely challenging.

I will walk you through the construction of a **Value Proposition that SELLS**, that speaks directly to your customers' needs, challenges, and goals in a way that is engaging, differentiated, quantifiable, and provable. There are several moving parts that we will need to gather before constructing it, and this plan will help you identify that information, and translate it into a **Value Proposition Platform** that can be used to deliver all the marketing and sales messaging needed to attract and win customers.

My goal is to teach you a simplified and repeatable process to create rock-solid value propositions for your existing and new offerings, and to extend it into product and service messaging, sales conversations, and marketing and sales materials. I look forward to sharing with you what my customers and I have learned together.

Lisa D. Dennis
President
Knowledgence Associates

www.valueproposition.expert
www.knowledgence.com

The Value Proposition Mirror

FROM THE RESEARCH: RELEVANCE RULES!

Almost all buyers (96%) in our survey ended up making a purchase from the vendor who prepared the most relevant value proposition that was aligned with the buyer's interests and needs. Buyers said that two-thirds of value propositions were relevant to their needs, but when we asked them for the vendors that they were considering, what was the lowest and highest value proposition relevance they experienced, the results were surprising. The highest level of relevance was only 71%, and the lowest was 30%. That's a wide range, but even more important is that notion that if the best that's out there is only 70% relevant to a buyer, then there is a real opportunity for anybody who increases relevance above that to stand out.

The Purpose of a Value Proposition

Determining what the value proposition is for our product or service can often be elusive. Typically, value propositions are developed from the "inside-out," with a focus on the product or service rather than the customer it is trying to attract. Getting clear on what value our organization's offerings deliver can depend on the point of view of different members of our team: product development, branding, sales, and product marketing. The bigger questions are first, determining what attracts a customer, and then what the story is that will most resonate with them.

Among the many marketing challenges and choices that must be made to effectively communicate our company's "story," the most important one is defining the value. What value does our company deliver? To whom is it delivered? How is our company's value communicated? These are key questions that require research and competitive review. But there is another crucial question that should come first, yet often gets skipped:

From whose perspective is value best described?

There is only one right answer to this question. Unfortunately, because we are all in love with our own product and services, it is frequently answered incorrectly. Most of us think the value proposition should be from the perspective of our own company and focused on our own products and services. It's our job to market and sell that. We use marketing language that is often couched in company-centric language instead of "buyer" language. The result: a value proposition that is just a thinly disguised advertisement of our product or service. The core message is centered on "here is what we have to sell and here is why you need to buy it," rather than keying into the primary concerns, needs, or issues of the buyer. This message forces the potential buyer to figure out on their own if our offer is a match, instead of making it easier to recognize our solution as the one they were looking for.

Let's look at a real example, pulled from a company website. It is very similar to many other value propositions out there.

EXAMPLE

> *We provide a full range of skills needed to direct and deliver a successful solution, including strategic direction, business analysis, management, system design, directory implementation, security assessment, application development and systems integration. We have developed a comprehensive, proven methodology, based on hundreds of engagements with Fortune 1000 clients in a wide range of industries. And our consultants average more than a decade of experience with the relevant technologies.*

Let's take a look at this value proposition a bit more critically. Every buyer-centric value proposition needs to answer the following three key questions:

1 What is the buyer trying to achieve, or solve, or fix?

2 What is the offer that our company has to address the buyer's specific needs?

3 Why would a buyer select our company over the other possible market alternatives (real and perceived)?

For this proposition to be meaningful in a customer interaction, these questions need to be answerable in specific terms. But it's hard to get traction with this example, isn't it?

The first question is the most difficult of all. We can speculate but there is nothing here that directly states the buyer challenge.

Question two is unclear as well. What is "the solution" they are referring to here? (It should be noted that this example was on the company's website, on a page proudly entitled "Our Value Proposition.")

The third question is not answered well either. How many of their competitors can claim the same differentiators?

The reason it's hard to get at specific answers is that, overall, the statement is very generic. And it's all about their organization – they are talking about themselves first, and the customer second. One quick test of a value proposition is to remove the company name, then have someone else look at it and try to figure out what the company does. Can they? A prospect may recognize the company name, and then fill in the blanks with their own knowledge or perceptions of what the company does. They could be right, or they could be wrong. Either way, the prospect must do the work here. By removing the company name, we can test if our value proposition is doing all the necessary work in communicating value to a prospect. They should not have to come up with the missing pieces on their own. And if they are not familiar with our company, they won't even try.

To summarize: our buyers want to hear about the value that our offer *delivers to them*, not the value of our offer. The difference is subtle but speaks to a primary weakness of most value propositions out there today. It must be outcome-based, not offer-based. Talking about features and benefits as part of a value proposition is missing the point of what a value proposition needs to be in today's market.

Sorting Out the Definitions

There are many value proposition definitions out there. There is also confusion about the difference between a *value proposition* and a *unique selling proposition* and an *elevator pitch.* They should all be connected, but they are not interchangeable. So, let's sort out these definitions.

Value Proposition (Standard Definition)

A value proposition is a clear and succinct statement indicating the specific value of a service or product or offer to a specific audience in order to differentiate its value.

Unique Selling Proposition

A unique selling proposition (USP, also known as unique selling point) is a factor that differentiates a product from its competitors, such as the lowest cost, the highest quality or the first-ever product of its kind. A USP could be thought of as "what we have that competitors don't."

Elevator Pitch

An elevator pitch (also known as an elevator speech, or elevator statement) is a short summary used to *quickly and simply* define a person / profession / product / service / organization and its value proposition. The name "elevator pitch" reflects the idea that it should be possible to deliver the summary in the time span of an elevator ride, or approximately thirty seconds to two minutes. The term itself comes from a scenario of an accidental meeting with someone important in the elevator.

As we can see, there are connections between them, but they are not the same. Both a USP and an Elevator Pitch rely on a solid value proposition, which seeks to communicate the value of the product or service offering. Features and functions are not enough. We must define the actual value delivered by the features and functions of an offering. Buyers are interested in outcomes. What will they experience, achieve, fix, or address?

In today's market place, buyers are expecting us to go further. We must define value from a true buyer point of view – not what **we** think they should value. That changes the very nature of what a value proposition needs to do.

Buyers are looking for a value proposition focused on their needs rather than the standard version which only talks about the Seller's products or services. Do we want them to engage early in their buyer journey? Or do we want to slug it out with competitors later in the game, when it's significantly harder to come up with a differentiated message amongst the noise of the other players?

Take a look at the next definition, which sets a new direction for value proposition development. Pay attention, and even read it a second time to identify what's truly different about it.

Buyer-Focused Value Proposition

> *A buyer-focused description of value that demonstrates your knowledge about the buyer's experience or challenge and your specific offer to address it, underscored by what differentiates your offer from any other.*

Figure out the difference? The major distinction is the point-of-view that is embedded in the value proposition. It's not about us or our offering. It's all about the *buyer*. It's about showing that we understand the buyer, that we have a clear picture of their experience (i.e. their challenge, issue, objective or goal). Our response to that experience is specific and relevant. It is differentiated by what truly makes our offer stand out from market alternatives. It is buyer-centric, which is a far more engaging way of attracting and retaining their attention.

The Mirror as a Value Proposition Metaphor

We need to shift our own perception of what a value proposition is, in order to better align ourselves with what the buyer needs. Let's think about the value proposition as being a mirror, the kind that each of us looks into every day!

Every time someone looks at a company – the website, the marketing content, listens to or reads the value proposition, talks to a sales person - they look in that mirror. Right now – today – what do they most often see? Is it your company's face or is it their own?

As business people, we typically think that our own "company face" should be there. Our organization is vested in talking about its own offer. And on many levels, that makes sense. But the reality is that buyers are trying to decide who is best suited to help them and who understands them the best. What they are seeking is their OWN face to be reflected in the "mirror" of our value proposition. That's right – they want to know that we understand and "get them." Their preference is that we can show a deep and informed understanding of their experience.

Seeing their own face reflected back at them is the most effective way to get that point across. The view must change from the typical "all about us and the stuff we want to sell you" approach to the one more favored by today's sophisticated buyer. We must *start* with the buyer in mind when we construct our statement.

We all know that the buyer is inundated with marketing messages galore from our competitors. Some of the solutions they are reviewing may not even be recognized as being viable alternatives. But that doesn't stop them from getting consideration. Both real and perceived competitors will be going head-to-head with us on our offering and messaging.

Comparison of features and benefits is increasingly not enough to get the upper hand. Standing out by talking about oneself has never been harder than it is today. How do we make our offer more attractive in the face of all that?

Here is the reality: companies who demonstrate true buyer knowledge within the context of their value propositions are rewarded with earlier engagement with their offerings, a better shot at being on the buyer's short list, and an increased likelihood of being chosen. As we mentioned at the beginning of this chapter, 96% of our surveyed buyers ended up making a purchase from the vendor who prepared the most relevant value proposition aligned with the buyer's interests and needs.

Becoming Buyer-Centric is All About Relevance

The key to vendor selection in today's buyer-controlled sales process is relevance. Our research study sheds some light on what matters to buyers, how it impacts their decisions, and what weaknesses they experience in the value propositions they consider. While this may seem obvious, it has unequivocal implications in how our offering is perceived throughout the buyers' journey. If we do not demonstrate relevance in the early stages, we will be disqualified long before we have an opportunity to engage. If it isn't relevant, go home!

How much of an issue is relevance in making buying decisions? Three out of every four respondents (76%) said that poor alignment of value propositions with buyer needs *significantly reduces a vendor's prospects for being recommended for the shortlist*, while 68% said it *reduces the likelihood of the offer being purchased*. Not only does relevance matter as a buyer gets acquainted with our offering, but also it must be sustained and expanded as the buyer moves through the complete buying process.

The first thing we need to do is gain a solid understanding of the types of value propositions that are in use, how each type differs, and the factors to consider as we begin to build or retool our value proposition approach. A lot of weak value propositions are out there – many more than strong ones. Why? Because creating a compelling value proposition is hard work! But there are some clear choices involved that will help us make informed decisions.

As mentioned earlier, most marketers never receive training on how to write a value proposition. We imitate others or use a format that the company has given us, or we look up "how to" on the Internet. These approaches can help in creating value propositions. But here's a thought: what if we let our buyer help us craft the right story?

VALUE POINTS

Buyer-centric value props must answer 3 key questions:

1   What is the buyer trying to achieve, or solve, or fix?

2   What is the offer that our company has to address the buyer's specific needs?

3   Why would a buyer select our company over the other possible market alternatives (both real and perceived)?

What is a buyer-focused value proposition?

A buyer-focused description of value that demonstrates our knowledge about the buyer's experience or challenge and our specific offer to address it, underscored by what differentiates our offer from any other.

When it's time to buy, members of the buying group pick their favorites based on which vendor has presented a value proposition most relevant to their needs.

If our value proposition does not align with buyer needs, most buyers won't recommend us for the shortlist or purchase our offer.

2

Choosing the Best Type

FROM THE RESEARCH: FOCUS ON THE BUYER!

Our respondents prefer a value proposition that is buyer-focused, addressing their needs, challenges and goals. A buyer-focused value proposition received a weight of 38% of 100%. A features and benefits focus, providing product and service details, was weighted at 35%, while a focus on alternatives (the vendor vs. competitors) was weighted only 27%. The respondents also predict that the importance of a buyer focus will increase as both the features/benefits focus and the alternatives focus diminish in importance to buyers.

So where do you as a marketing person start your value proposition development? Here is what usually happens: pick the audience targets, then starting writing about features and benefits. Keep writing about features and benefits. Talk about how we have the only solution (with no proof) and add that we have excellent customer service. The End.

It is true that most marketing people start with the product or service description. The task at hand is to highlight those features that speak to the buyer types we have selected, and then draft accompanying benefits that our teams can use to market and sell. Sounds simple and direct, right? But wait!

What if there is another decision to be made BEFORE we start the writing process? There is a very big decision that can determine the strength and flexibility of our value proposition. We need to be able to have the value proposition stand up both in marketing communications and sales conversations. The best way to achieve this goal is to start with the end in mind. As we know, the end is having a buyer say "yes" at the closure of a marketing and sales process. Yet, one of the biggest challenges in reaching that goal is the creation of a solid message that works well not only across all available marketing communications channels, but also in the field with sales people to enable them to engage and deliver our offering's story in a way that resonates with buyers. Many organizations land at the same place in their efforts to build their story. An unhappy, unsatisfactory, divided place where Marketing is presenting one message and Sales is frequently saying something different.

The Classic Sales and Marketing Debate

If you are from Sales, do you ever feel that the messaging you get from Marketing doesn't quite have the punch that you need to have a great sales conversation? Many sales people would unequivocally say YES! The message and the language might play well in marketing collateral, or on the website, or in a piece of digital content, but they don't translate well to an actual conversation that a buyer is willing to engage in.

Many sellers end up taking a step beyond marketing messages by creating language and talk tracks that will open the door and build to an ongoing sales conversation. Typically, sales people do this independently, driven by the necessity to break through to their prospects in whatever way they can. Multiply this by the number of sales people on your team, and you will quickly get an idea of how many ways the core message can be altered and potentially fractured.

In Marketing, the challenge and frustration is that crafting a strong value proposition and building messaging is a complex process. The value proposition "platform" needs to accomplish each of these objectives:

- Reflect accurately the key aspects of the product or service.

- Account for, and respond appropriately to, industry trends and dynamics.

- Consider and address competitive offerings and their value propositions.

- Differentiate the offer in a way that stands out to buyers.

- Provide the foundation for a strong, repeatable story that can be integrated into all external communication vehicles.

- Serve up the right message to the sales team so they are communicating both the substance and the story accurately and consistently to your company's markets.

This is a tall order when Sales frequently changes up the message. They bend it, invert it, extend it, and even embroider it to get a prospect's attention. In their defense, they are simply trying to find a message that "sticks" with their target prospects. Except by doing this, the value proposition story becomes inconsistent with the overall brand and product/service messaging that you have made great efforts to develop. At the end of the day, Sales must engage in value-based conversations to get buyers to pick our offering. If the "value" isn't embedded in the messaging, they have no choice but to change it.

This is a common occurrence across B2B organizations. It happens when Marketing doesn't involve Sales in the process of creating the value proposition. But another major factor that contributes to this debate is in the actual type of value proposition that is used to construct the messaging. There are three basic types of value propositions to choose from. However, most organizations default to just one type. This happens because most marketers don't realize that there are other options. There are some significant differences between the value proposition types, and the choice itself can have a major impact on the output of our development work.

Let's walk through the three types of value propositions to get a solid understanding of the pros and cons of each. We'll look at an example of each type to see each one in action.

Offer Driven: The "Inside-Out" Value Proposition

This option represents the standard approach that many companies adopt when they are developing their messaging. It is the type of value proposition that organizations recognize. It reflects the product/service orientation that many companies have and that drive most marketing and sales activities, and it's the default type that most marketing people use. It focuses on our own company and its products and services. It has an inside-out orientation which doesn't typically factor in the buyer's perspective and language in its approach.

Competitor Driven: The "Us versus Them" Value Proposition

The second option shifts the focus from inside the company to outside, looking at key competitors. Like the offer driven approach, this one focuses on company, products and service, but it strives to respond to a prime competitor or group of competitors. Where there is tough competition or confusion in the market about who the leader is, or what the key offering attributes are, this approach aims to differentiate. It presents what our company has that the other player(s) in our space do not. On the face of it, this is an improvement over the default type because it does have more of an exterior view. However, the primary focus again is on product or service, which often results in a feature / benefit war. Given that most features – even the most innovative – have a shelf life in terms of actual differentiation; it is a never-ending task to stay on top of what the competitors are doing, and how we stack up against them. It becomes like a chess match against our best competitors. The big problem is that it leaves the buyer on the sidelines as an *audience*, rather than as a key player in the conversation.

Buyer-Driven: The "It's All About the Buyer" Value Proposition

The final option puts the focus where it should be: on the buyers themselves. This approach directly addresses issues, challenges, goals and objectives of concern to the buyers. It speaks to what is top-of-mind to a buyer: ways to solve a problem or provide a solution or enable a goal, not the details of a business offering. The messaging and language used reflect the buyers' context, words and intentions. This is the *best* choice of value proposition for a host of reasons – not the least of which is that it's the only one where the buyers will see their faces reflected in the mirror of your value proposition.

A Deeper Look at the Components of Choice

Fundamentally, developing statements of value for our offerings is not an easy thing to do. We face a series of decisions as we narrow down to a message that resonates with our buyers. For each of the value proposition types, many considerations go into making an informed decision. Here are just a few:

- What key question will we answer?

- What direction will we take?

- What components will we include?

- What is our primary approach?

- How difficult is it to compose?

Type 1: Offer-Driven (Inside-Out)

This type of value proposition answers an important question that we assume every potential buyer will ask. It is a very familiar "marketing 101" question, which is not to say that the question itself isn't important. However, the challenge with it is that it can generate a broad range of potential responses.

Key Question: Why should I buy your product or service?

What direction should we take in answering this question to get the best response from the right targets? The possibilities have the potential to overwhelm our buyer. At a minimum, there are as many paths to an offer message as there are features in our offering. Let's break down the Offer-Driven approach, and some of the challenges of this type of value proposition. The primary stage of the buying process is when product/service knowledge is of relatively high importance.

Decisions	Your Choice	Challenges
What direction will you take?	Demonstrate Thorough Product / Service Knowledge	Based on product-centric assumptions
What components will you include?	List all benefits delivered by the offering	Features and benefits are often confused
What is your primary approach?	Lots of benefits equals value	Not all benefits may be important for the buyer
How hard is it to compose?	Easiest type to construct	Doesn't involve much customer insight
Relevant Buying Stage:	Awareness	

This approach relies heavily on product and service knowledge as the core of the message. It's the easiest value proposition to build because its contents are readily available and familiar. Identifying the benefits is a key step. But this is an area that requires careful consideration, as there is often the temptation to create and communicate as many benefits as possible as a means of demonstrating value. More benefits do not automatically equal more value.

A product-centric view can create a set of assumptions about what is important to our buyers. Put another way, it has the potential to focus on what *we* think is important, which may or may not resonate for the buyer. Also, the feature / benefit definition is challenging. Typically, there is not enough clarity on the differences between a feature and a benefit, and how they should consistently connect and support each other. In complex product offerings, this confusion is widespread. Furthermore, a wealth of benefits does not necessarily guarantee value in the eyes of the buyer. Not all benefits are equal, and many may not be important enough for the buyer to decide in our favor.

With more complex offerings, value proposition development efforts of this type struggle with clarity on which features and functionality are specifically included in the offer. In the name of differentiation, benefits get created that may need to be traced back and verified as being accurate, not to mention relevant to the actual product. This is a clear symptom of an inward-focused approach to defining value. I have sat in meetings with product marketing managers and listened to them debate if the benefits they want to add to the messaging actually relate or tie back to any of the features. There is often a lack of clarity on the exact features when the offering is highly complex. How do you write something that buyers will understand and engage with if you aren't clear yourself about it? It happens all the time!

Ultimately, construction of this type of value proposition doesn't require knowing a lot about the buyer, which is an inherent weakness in its construction.

Offer-Driven Value Proposition Examples

Looking at some actual examples will illustrate the "inside-out" nature of this kind of value proposition. These examples are all from real companies. As you review them, see if it is possible to identify anything that relates to a buyer type, and/or their needs and challenges.

Global Professional Services Provider

> *"We Accelerate Growth." Our partnership is based around the objective of growth. In order to help you grow, it is paramount that you connect and interact with our global network of experts at all levels. Involvement is the key. All relevant decision-makers from your company must become involved and interact with the entire XYZ Corporation global team.*

Healthcare Company

We deliver healthcare through an efficient, integrated and accountable delivery model that brings the best value with the following attributes:

- *A strategic partnership between the health plan and health system.*

- *As consumers, employers can now buy healthcare on value, including differentiated price.*

- *Innovative use of technology and integrated healthcare data management.*

- *Efficient infrastructure for population health management and patient advocacy.*

- *Metrics drive future transformation of healthcare for all stakeholders.*

- *Health plan and health system share with you the financial accountability for your healthcare costs.*

- *Value drives future financing of healthcare needs for you and your employees.*

Manufacturer

> *Our biggest advantage comes from the fact that XYZ Company is a one-stop solutions provider. Vertical integration coupled with a proven end to end manufacturing/availability model adds synergies to business. In an industry that is fragmented, we offer a comprehensive range of products and services that covers all aspects of SSL solutions, i.e. from conceptualization to actualization. Creating value together with our partners and customers is perhaps the most key value for all.*
>
> *We, however, do not simply stop at the manufacture and assembly of products. At XYZ Company we make sure that our products are working properly for you. For this reason, we also offer a Total Manufacturing System wherein the performance of products manufactured are tested and analyzed for maximum efficiency. Over the years, we have gained a reputation as a problem solver, confronting the issues of our customers and providing the right solutions.*

Some core weaknesses that are emblematic of a product / service focused value proposition are inherent in these examples. The largest issue is the lack of context with the buyer's experience, which forces buyers into figuring out for themselves how the offering stands in relation to their needs. From a marketing perspective, this is problematic. A buyer's attention span is short, and they may be sifting through dozens of competing messages. From a sales perspective, it is challenging because communicating the value of the offering is largely unaddressed within the value proposition statement itself, leaving Sales to figure out on their own how to have a value-based conversation.

Consider this: a clear statement that does *not* include buyer-centric value can disqualify an offering during the buyer's journey before sales people even get an opportunity to engage. For as we've learned:

> *Customers engage suppliers relatively late in the purchase process: The average purchase decision is 57% complete, and more than 10 information sources have been consulted, by the time customers engage with suppliers. Alarmingly, the higher the purchase complexity, the later customers engage suppliers.*

CEB, 5 Customer Buying Trends You Can't Ignore, 2015

Couple that statistic (which has been widely quoted and has had a significant impact on both marketing and sales strategy), with the nature of how the buyer's journey is conducted in B2B markets today:

> *67 percent of the buyer's journey is now done digitally. Search/web exploration is the first course of action for executives.*

Sirius Decisions, CXO Study, 2013

The weaknesses inherent in an offer-centric statement increasingly have become an issue for companies trying to attract and engage B2B buyers and bring them to a closed sale. The weaknesses center on two key factors: the information a buyer needs; and the most essential factors or value drivers that a buyer considers before putting our company on the short list for a decision.

Weaknesses

- No information about buyer challenges, issues, needs or pains

- Lack of specifics on actual value delivered (expressed in dollar amounts or percentages)

- Generic language applicable to any business in any industry

- Features disguised as benefits

- Internally focused and company-centric

- No demonstrable or provable differentiators

Type 2: Competitor-Driven (Us versus Them)

For fifty years, Avis promised "We Try Harder," a direct comparison to their primary auto rental competitor, Hertz. Its strength was in acknowledging the competition and then focusing on the way they, themselves, added value to the driver experience. This type of value proposition strives to answer:

> *Key Question: Why should I buy your product or service instead of your competitor's?*

From the buyer's perspective, this is a better question than the offer-driven question, as it recognizes the reality that our buyer is comparing us with other alternatives in the market. However, it still is product / service focused. It compares features and benefits head to head. Often, the value proposition will concentrate on the one or two things that the competitor doesn't have or doesn't do well. Although this improves upon the Offer-Driven approach, there is still no clear sign of the potential buyer in the mirror! In this situation, knowledge of alternatives is most important at the Preference stage of the Buyers' Journey.

Decisions	Your Choice	Challenges
What direction will you take?	Acknowledge market alternatives	May miss "perceived" alternatives
What components will you include?	Product / service knowledge	Still doesn't require much buyer insight
What is your primary approach?	Requires detailed information on competitor offerings to identify clear differentiators	Don't know which differentiators are material to the buyer
How hard is it to compose?	More effort required to construct	Need reliable competitor information
Relevant Buying Stage:	Preference	

It is always an important exercise to evaluate our offers head-to-head against our competitors. So, beyond the baseline of our own product and service knowledge, getting detailed intelligence on competitor offerings is vital for this type. We need to understand in depth how their product or service is constructed, and where the gaps or opportunities exist for us to position against them.

We also need a clear view of our competitor's buyer audience and the message they are delivering to that audience about their offerings. There is a risk here in latching on to a product deficiency and building our message entirely around that. It is wise not to bet the house on any feature that is not patented or otherwise protected, as this will be a short-term advantage at best. Not to mention, this tactic does not protect us from superior messaging that sidesteps or diminishes the importance of our differentiating feature.

The bigger challenge is that in hyper-focusing on a single or small group of competitors, we may miss another company that our buyers perceive to be a viable alternative (whether we believe or acknowledge that, or not). These periphery players can possibly chip away at our stance if we don't identify them and factor them in.

Netting out our position versus the others ultimately depends on the differentiators we set out as our basis for being chosen. A head-to-head approach can result in a variety of differentiators. Without actual insights from buyers, how will we decide which ones are most meaningful to them? If we don't have a strong understanding of our buyer's situation, challenges, goals, and pains, we will have to assume which areas of our offer are the most relevant in the context of the buyer's experience. This is a risky approach if there is any uncertainty about the accuracy of those assumptions. And the buyers may still have to filter through all the differentiators to find the one or two that matter to them. Even riskier, this type of value proposition tends to have too many differentiators that are not provable or demonstrable or are so vague as to render them meaningless. Defining a true, provable differentiator is hard – especially doing it without buyer insights clearly in mind.

Competitor-Driven Value Proposition Examples

Of the three types, this one sees the lowest adoption rate by companies. Where there are many competitors, most organizations focus on a product / service offer and seek to highlight that. However, it can be effective if pitched against a well-defined, small group, or a clear head-to-head position against competitors. Look at some actual examples that will illustrate the "us versus them" nature of this kind of value proposition. These examples are all samples from real companies. Again, see if it is possible to identify anything that relates to a buyer type and/or their needs and challenges.

Software Provider

> Service-oriented architecture (SOA) helps government agencies respond quickly to the needs of their citizens and day to day operations by providing a suite of tools to fully enable and automate disparate applications and business processes. The key to success in government lies beyond creating the ability to respond to opportunities and threats. You also must identify them as early as possible to drive your business vision to a successful delivery of product and service leadership. SOA allows you to do so by opening the integration and automation of the value chain.

> Despite the significant progress made with open standards in the industry, most SOA platforms are delivered with proprietary, closed extensions that focus on customer lock-in more than automation of the value chain.

> We believe there is a better way. We redefine SOA as simple, open and affordable. Many agencies and institutions are already realizing the benefits of XYZ Company's product, our open source portfolio offering for SOA. These products lay the foundation for XYZ Company to provide even greater support excellence, customer deployment experiences, and satisfaction.

In addition to this statement, the company also used a graphic that compared itself directly to three other competitors on the key differentiator of Customer Satisfaction and quantified their position with third party proof. In some respects, this is a hybrid of a Type 2 value proposition (Competitor-Driven) and a Type 3 (Buyer-Driven). Consider the strengths and weaknesses of this example:

Strengths

- References a buyer challenge with comparable offers

- Quantifies the value by providing an objective 3rd party rating

- Uses industry relevant language

- Offer statements connect directly to buyer challenge

- Differentiator comparison to alternatives with objective proof

Weakness

- Assumes that customer satisfaction is the most important differentiator.

- While it is an advantage as presented, how relevant or important is that to the overall decision process for one of their solutions?

- Every business has satisfied customers at some level. This can potentially be a "generic" differentiator unless there is objective, third party proof that gives it some teeth.

Type 3: Buyer-Driven (It's All About the Buyer)

This type of value proposition puts the buyer up front and seeks to communicate value from their point of view. It recognizes that buyers are trying to net out everything they have learned about available offerings in order to make an informed and focused choice. In effect, this is a refinement of what matters most to our intended targets.

Key Question: What are the most important things for me to consider in my decision-making process?

This is a higher-order question that represents the process that every buyer goes through as they research and evaluate options to address their needs. In the first two types of value propositions presented above, the onus is on the buyer to do the work to get to an answer to this question. But if we cut to the chase and provide the answer up front, we've gone a long way towards getting the buyer's attention early.

Of the three types, the **Buyer-Driven Value Proposition** asks the most effective question to attract and engage buyers, because it inherently answers both Question 1 and Question 2, while couching them in terms that are most relevant to the buyer's needs.

Decisions	Your Choice	Challenges
What direction will you take?	• Focus on customer-defined values • Identify key points of difference	• Needs to be simple, but powerful • Need to know what matters most to buyer
What components will you include?	• Product / service knowledge • Detailed information on competitor offerings to differentiate • Values to the customer	• Needs to be put in customer language • Focus only on the differentiator(s) that can be quantified
What is your primary approach?	Requires defining value to customer	Value must be provable
How hard is it to compose?	Most effort required to construct	Net out to customer needs / issues / challenges
Relevant Buying Stage:	Consideration	

Clearly, we must work harder to craft this type of value proposition. But it yields many advantages, the foremost of which is that it will resonate with buyers sooner and more deeply than any other version. Sellers work hard to redefine Offer-Driven value propositions to get to language that encourages a buyer to engage with them. The key point here is that we must be crystal clear on what our buyer actually values. Not only do we need to understand exactly what is different and comparable about our offer, we must also understand what parts of it may be difficult for the buyer to grasp, which could create uncertainty in their minds. This knowledge will allow you to nail the answer when the buyer asks that all-important question, "What is the most important thing for me to consider?" This type of value proposition is most relevant during "Consideration," the final stage of the buyer's journey prior to making a decision to buy.

Examples

Technology Company

> *For IT organizations wrestling with the high cost and inflexibility of the old "one server, one application" model, XYZ Corporation can improve the efficiency and availability of IT resources and applications through virtualization. About 70% of a typical IT budget in a non-virtualized datacenter goes towards just maintaining the existing infrastructure, with little left for innovation. XYZ Corporation can free our IT admins from spending so much time managing servers rather than innovating. An automated datacenter built on the production-proven XYZ Corporation virtualization platform lets us respond to market dynamics faster and more efficiently than ever before. XYZ customers typically save 50-70% on overall IT costs by consolidating their resource pools and delivering highly available machines with XYZ product.*

Healthcare Company

Employers, insurers and claims paying organizations are rightly concerned with the increased costs of their workers' compensation, group health, and auto liability programs – but their cost control efforts may not generate the desired goal.

XYZ Company's Response to These Client and Market Needs

We have focused our healthcare and professional services resources, along with our technology, information system and work process re-engineering expertise to create and deliver the following business benefits and results:

- *Improved cost efficiencies for providing claims and patient services*

- *Increased speed and quality of decision-making and communication*

- *Increased service consistency and reliability*

- *Increased accuracy and authority of information*

- *Increased cost savings delivered to our clients*

- *Increased frequency of superior outcomes for our patients.*

Wholesale Distributor

Nothing can give us more joy than finding a new exceptional and unique coffee, establishing a close relationship with a farmer or a coffee community, and having a positive social or environmental impact while we do what we love. Nothing can be more challenging than the details of managing the supply chain and monitoring farms, in a foreign country, with limited time and resources. And if you want to compete in the roasting market today, the supply chain challenges are unavoidable if you are on your own.

We can help you find quality coffees and bring you closer to the farmer, while managing the supply chain at origin and the ongoing monitoring of farms for you. Our value proposition is simple, we let you focus on what you need to focus on, finding great coffees and ensuring a consistent, dependable supply.

This is our offering:

- *Fine quality coffees from Honduras for unique blends, estate coffees, and espressos*

- *Solid established relationships in Honduras with leading exporters, farms, cooperatives, and institutions*

- *Significant savings of resources and costs associated with the development of farm relationships*

- *Sustainability programs at origin and full traceability*

- *Social responsibility and fair business practices*

- *Proximity of supply leading to reliable, short delivery times, and a carbon-efficient supply chain*

- *Focused attention on a single origin*

As mentioned earlier, most weak value propositions are focused only on the product or service. They are weak because the buyer's needs, challenges and insights are not typically embedded, which leaves connecting the dots up to the buyer. They must figure out if the offer can address their needs, and if that requires too much effort, they will move on to other alternatives without a second look. The more benefits we try to tout, the more challenging we make it for them to sort things out. The buyer-centric examples above include the following:

Strengths

- Each includes specific buyer needs, challenges, issues, or pains

- Each uses industry relevant language

- The offer statements connect directly to the buyer experience

- Each takes a buyer-focused approach

- The differentiators are focused on outcomes that buyers desire

Weaknesses

- Additional quantification is needed to provide the buyer with key data that demonstrates value in real terms (numbers, percentages, statistics)

- Differentiators need proof also (numbers, percentages, statistics and third-party endorsements or customer results)

Less is More in Value Proposition Statements

The key to creating a strong value proposition lies squarely in talking only about what matters to targeted buyers. Don't be afraid to be specific, because we aren't trying to sell to everyone. Not everyone is a viable prospect for our product or services. Casting a wide net with a more generic message that tries to appeal to everyone decreases our ability to find and attract those who will make a decision in our favor and buy.

There are quite a few weak value propositions out there – many more than strong ones. Why? Because doing this is not easy! But there are some clear choices involved that will help you craft a better approach, instead of simply copying what every other company is doing.

Most marketers never receive any training on how to write a value proposition. We imitate others or use a format that the company has given us, or we look up "how to" on the internet. All are basically viable options that are in practice everywhere. But the vast majority of them produce mediocrity that leaves all parties involved feeling unfulfilled.

While the **Buyer-Driven Value Proposition** type takes the most effort, it provides the most solid and engaging platform to create messaging that will resonate with our buyer audience. Further, it helps deliver a sales-enabled message to both inside and field sales teams, decreasing the likelihood they will make it up, or dramatically change the message in an effort to find something that will hook a prospect.

VALUE POINTS

The **Offer-Driven Value Proposition** focuses on the seller's own company and products and services. It has an inside-out orientation which doesn't typically factor in the buyer's perspective and language in its approach.

The **Competitor-Driven Value Proposition** compares features and benefits head to head with specific competitors. It typically concentrates on the one or two things that are different or better than the competitor(s). It is still product / service focused, the crux of which may or may not be relevant to the buyer.

The **Buyer-Driven Value Proposition** approach places the buyer first, in terms of their issues, challenges, goals, and objectives. It aims to solve a problem or provide a solution or enable a goal that is more top-of-mind to a buyer than the offering's details. The messaging and language is geared directly to the buyer audience in their context, words, and intentions.

3

Creating the Value Proposition Platform™

FROM THE RESEARCH: ALIGN WITH THE BUYER'S NEEDS!

Our respondents made it clear that the "relevance" they sought was defined by "alignment with their interests and needs." In fact, 93% percent reported that some vendors were able to present value propositions better aligned with their needs than others. And they validated that point by reporting that almost all of them (96%) purchased from the vendor who offered the most relevant value propositions aligned with their interests and needs.

As we begin to build a value proposition, there are some key decisions to make and steps that we need to take. The first is to decide on the type of value proposition we will create. Based on the research point above, we should go with the "Buyer-Focused Type" as it, by definition, has the orientation we will need to more closely align with our buying audience. We will need to research and understand what our competition is saying to our buyers, as well. It's likely they also are not that well-aligned, thus providing real opportunities for us to create messaging that will stand out. Most importantly, we'll have to clear away a lot of noise to focus on what's most important in aligning with the varied interests and needs of different buyers. That's why we may need several versions of our value proposition.

Extended Examples for this Book: MediaConvo, Inc. and Top Line Sales

To help this process come alive for you, we examine two "real life" company examples throughout the book, to demonstrate how real people translated these concepts and instructions into value propositions, and how they used their value propositions to strengthen their sales and marketing initiatives. I engaged with each of these companies throughout their entire value proposition development.

MediaConvo was a real company for which I conducted a marketing message strategy project that included developing what came to be five versions of the value proposition. Since this project was completed several years ago, the company has been sold twice and now ceases to exist within its former structure, name, or leadership. Nevertheless, for the purposes of this book, I have changed the company name, product names, and all competitor names from my notes. (There is consistency, though; whenever you see "Competitor C", for example, it always represents the same company.)

MediaConvo was a software technology company selling a product in a wide variety of industries, to at least two distinct buyer groups: Marketers and Public Relations professionals. They were delivering a growing range of services along with their product, but struggling with their corporate identity.

I chose this example for several reasons. First, I have detailed examples of research that I conducted on their behalf, so you can see the information we gathered and learned from, in order to hone in on strong messages. Secondly, I will share multiple restatements of their value propositions in progress, as we iterated the message and gathered internal and external feedback. This will demonstrate how we made improvements to get closer to themes, ideas, and language that reflected the buyers needs and wants.

Top Line Sales is the real name of a strategic sales consulting, training, and large account coaching company in Portland, Oregon, owned by Lisa Magnuson. Lisa recently engaged me to help her create a value proposition for her company. She has graciously allowed me to use all her materials in this book, along with illustrations of some of the business development, sales and marketing changes she has made since completing the project. Lisa's value proposition has not only changed how she presents to her clients and prospects, but quite literally has transformed her entire business. This example will illustrate a service company rather than a product company, a small rather than larger company, and a very different research method.

The Value Proposition Platform™

My **Value Proposition Platform** is a two-page summary statement of the key elements of a single version of a value proposition. Typically, we will need a main value proposition, focused on a specific offering with our primary target audience. But we may also need to fine-tune that for other targets and for different industries as well. The business issues could be different; the language or market imperatives could be different. So, we need to be prepared to take our foundational value proposition, and create additional versions as needed. We'll produce a similar format for each version that we need. Let's take a look at the final versions of our two example companies.

Top Line Sales		Version: VP of Sales	Value Proposition Platform	
SECTOR: Technology	**PRIMARY INDUSTRY**	Information Technology companies and other B2B companies	**SEGMENTS:**	Technology, software (SaaS), storage & peripherals, manufacturing, printing, healthcare, services
TARGET	**DECISION MAKER TITLES:**	VP Sales, VP of Sales and Marketing, Director of Sales CEO, Business Owner	**INFLUENCER TITLES:**	N/A
BUSINESS ISSUES	1 Our sales results are not good enough. 2 I don't have time to focus on strategic account development. 3 My team lacks skills to pursue, close, expand and retain large accounts. 4 We don't do a good job of differentiating from the competition. 5 My team is inconsistent in landing larger deals.			

VALUE PROPOSITION STATEMENT

BUYER OBJECTIVE	When was the last time each of your team members closed a seven-figure contract? Despite the best sales talent, many high potential, critical deals get whittled down or are lost completely. Large opportunities are complex and require a carefully orchestrated approach to identify, develop and win.
COMPANY OFFER	We overcome the barriers to winning TOP Line Accounts™ whether they're worth 100K or 10M+. Top Line Sales instills the know-how into your sales organization to identify, cultivate and close strategic account opportunities through a field-proven process that includes the right tools, strategic training and live deal coaching. Our war room service ensures that your most important account opportunities have the highest level of focus, accountability and momentum all the way through closure. This directed approach increases critical contract close ratios, and turns your sales team into strategic, "Top Line" sellers.
DIFFERENTIATOR	Our clients boast of closed contracts totaling over $100 million in new revenue due to our commitment to 'roll up our sleeves' to help your team win. We are not simply 'advice givers' - we work side-by-side with your account executives, running strategic opportunity war rooms, applying just-in-time expertise and arming them with tools and live coaching where it counts: in the field.

Top Line Sales	Version: VP of Sales	Value Proposition Platform
VALUE DRIVERS	**QUANTIFICATION**	**PROOF**
Improved close ratios of big deals	Fortune 50 Manufacturing Client Case: $25m deal, largest in company that year	"Because of our relationship with Top Line Sales, sales management now has a clear line of sight between sales goals and revenue results." Sandy Barnes, Cameron Design Group
Sales growth	High Tech Client Case: six-fold increase in 'million-dollar' deals over the past year alone	This approach has translated into greater consistency, meaning fewer valleys and higher peaks in the volume of closed sales." Mark M. Fallon, President & CEO, The Berkshire Company
Retain and grow largest accounts	Healthcare Insurance Client Case: Retained multi-million $ client through RFP Rebid	"The investment will have far reaching returns with improving our sales conversation, consistently understanding the customer's point of view, improved confidence of our sales people and retention of our most important and strategic customers." Jeni Billups, Senior VP, Sales & Marketing, Oregon Freeze Dry

MediaConvo, Inc.		Version: Marketing	Value Proposition Platform	
SECTOR: Technology	**PRIMARY INDUSTRY**	Information Technology	**SEGMENTS:**	Technology Hardware, Software, and Peripherals
TARGET	**DECISION MAKER TITLES:**	Chief Marketing Officer, VP Marketing, VP Product Marketing, Director of Analyst Relations	**INFLUENCER TITLES:**	Marketing Manager, Public Relations Manager, Analyst Relations Manager, Public Relations Agency, Product Manager

BUSINESS ISSUES	1 Need to know what customers are thinking and what trends are in a timely manner.
	2 Content about our brand is being created by people external to our company and we don't always know what they are saying.
	3 Traditional media research tools are not effective for consumer-generated media.
	4 Must prove to senior executives that we are being successful.
	5 Protect corporate reputation by understanding impact of our brand in all our markets.
	6 Don't have a standardized and automated way to collect mentions—very labor intensive pulling from multiple systems and individual research.

VALUE PROPOSITION STATEMENT

BUYER OBJECTIVE	Tuning into the voice of your market is becoming more difficult due to the millions of consumer-to-consumer conversations that are diluting the impact of your company's marketing programs. In today's Influence 2.0 world, consumers are creating their own brand dialog by blending your product messaging with their own experiences and opinions, other consumers' input, and traditional media content. Can you afford to be out of sync with your market?
COMPANY OFFER	MediaConvo, a market influence analytics company, sifts and interprets the millions of voices at the intersection of consumer-generated and traditional media. Our award-winning platform, Opus, integrates innovative technology with expert analysis to identify the people, issues and trends impacting your business—at the speed of the market.
DIFFERENTIATOR	MediaConvo pioneered a proprietary content analysis engine to extract meaning from high volumes and diverse sources of text, a technology used by U.S. intelligence agencies for over 8 years. We are an innovator in the integration of consumer-generated media and mainstream media, offering access to the greatest breadth of content sources and analytical expertise available in the market.

MediaConvo, Inc.	Version: CMO, VP Sales	Value Proposition Platform
VALUE DRIVERS	**QUANTIFICATION**	**PROOF**
Immediacy	"Best of Show" - Massachusetts Innovation Technology Exchange, for Best Use of Technology and Applied Technology - for delivering immediate market intelligence	"Allows our PR teams to dynamically adjust campaigns based on what is happening now – not what happened three months ago." Fleishman Hillard
Relevance	For marketing professionals, measurement is a crucial focus. Katie Paine of KD Paine & Partners states: "I think measurement is our key to credibility and power. The more we base decisions on solid data and not on gut instinct, the more people in the C-Suite will pay attention to what we have to say."	"At TRW, we needed a standardized way to measure our mentions and key message pickup to assist in providing valid data to management about the success of our media relations efforts relative to competitors." TRW
Proof	The importance of consumer online activity has been steadily increasing. A survey conducted by Jupiter Research revealed: "66 percent of surveyed companies are operating under the assumption that the effect of consumer-created content on brands will greatly increase over the next 12 months."	"MediaConvo is offering innovative market intelligence solutions that allow its clients to accurately measure and analyze media coverage, market leadership and corporate reputation in real-time." KM World

The first section focuses on which **SECTOR** we are aiming at and identifies the **primary industry and industry segments** for the value proposition. If our product or service offering is aimed at different industries, it will be necessary to create additional versions of the **Value Proposition Platform** to ensure that our messaging is industry- and segment-relevant.

The next section is focused on the **TARGETS** we are aiming at, identified as the **titles of key decision makers** and those who typically **influence** their decisions at companies in these industry segments.

The third section focuses on key **BUSINESS ISSUES** that our company knows are significant to the decision-makers and influencers, as well as relevant to our offering. The business issues must be discussed from the point of view of the target audience. This section is **not** about the issues that our product or service solves. An outside-in perspective is needed here – outside our company, from *their* world, in *their* language.

Together, these three sections above identify the value proposition audience. To achieve true relevance, we must be crystal clear in this section, and we must learn or figure out the nature of the issues, goals, or problems they seek to solve, given a relevant and appropriate solution.

The **Value Proposition Statement** itself consists of three parts:

1   **The Buyer Objective**: A statement (in the words of the buyers) about what they hope to accomplish, or are struggling with, or need to address in their own business. This needs to be completely from the buyer's viewpoint, in their language. This statement should be entirely about them.

2   **The Company Offer**: The best, concise statement of our product / service that *specifically addresses* the Buyer Objective Statement. It is designed to be a response to the

needs stated in the Buyer Objective Statement. This is our first opportunity to connect the buyer's needs to our offer. It is also very important that our offer is communicated in their language, rather than using internal company-speak.

3 **The Differentiator**: One or more provable points of differentiation from key competitors that are both relevant and important to these buyers' objectives. Keep in mind that more differentiators do not automatically equate to more value. Relevance and proof here is critical.

Finally, there are three additional sections that make your value proposition bullet-proof. This is almost always missing from most of value props out there – whether they are business-to-business, or business-to-consumer.

4 **Value Drivers**: Our selection of the three primary value points that are typically top-of-mind for the buyers, and which drive them to action. These drivers allow us to extend, validate and demonstrate our differentiation.

5 **Quantification**: Quantifiable back-up of our differentiators and value drivers. Our buyers will pay attention and respond when there is clear and objective back-up to our claims.

6 **Proof**: Backing up the value prop in the form of testimonials, expert sources, and other credible and objective third-party validation.

Your Value Proposition Project

Whether your value proposition work or re-work is a stand-alone project or part of a larger marketing activity (such as a brand audit, a re-branding, a positioning platform or a new corporate identity), the most important thing you can do up front is to have a senior marketing or sales leader in your organization who is solidly behind the effort.

Maybe *you* are the executive sponsor for this project. If so, take the time to make a good case to enlist the support of other key stakeholder colleagues, such as Product Marketing, Product Development, Brand Marketing, Sales Leadership, Public Relations, and your own team. If you are a small or medium size business, ask yourself who on your team needs to be part of this?

Getting input from people who develop or deliver your offering, and those who market and sell it, will be crucial. Get input from your customers also. We need both internal AND external input to build something that is strong, compelling, and differentiating. If you head up the team that is responsible for value proposition language, you can save yourself and your team a lot of heartbreak by getting the internal support you need before beginning this project.

Either way, you cannot, and must not, do this under the radar. Developing it alone, without internal input and without external input from valued customers or partners, is a recipe for failure. There are people within your organization who will need to work with and use the value proposition. If their input is not part of the mix, they will ignore it and create their own on-the-fly, or else they will simply improvise changes to yours and use it in the field – thereby delivering a different message that can and will be confusing to your target audience.

You or your champion should enlist some enthusiasm from the sales team; make it a win for them from the get-go. If you have a sales-enablement function in Marketing or Sales or elsewhere in your organization, that person or team should be your new best friend on a project like this. If they're into playbooks, you'll be providing lots of good new pages!

Some Opening Advice

In the coming chapters, we are going to dive deep into each of these sections and explore exactly how you can go about creating remarkable value propositions for your own company. But first, let's look at some general hints, including some "dos and don'ts."

It isn't always easy to determine what should be included in a value proposition and what should be used elsewhere in marketing and sales materials. The tendency is to stuff the value proposition with as many features and benefits as you can, like "stuffing the ballot box." This is problematic because a greater number of features and benefits do not automatically translate into values that are relevant to prospects and customers. Think about your car for a moment. It has features galore. Now, how many of them do you use? How many of them are important to you? All of them? I doubt it!

Here are some attributes to concentrate on, and to make certain are represented in the value proposition.

- Center on the buyer's experience, not the product or service.

- Use buyer language, not internal "company-speak."

- Communicate key benefits of value to the buyer, not every product or service benefit you can think of.

- Focus on uniqueness and specifics, not generalities.

- Cover both qualitative and quantitative factors.

- Limit your differentiators to the one or two things that are unique or better.

- Make sure it's believable and demonstrable.

- Offer objective, credible proof of your claims.

Every potential customer has some drivers that will guide their purchasing behavior. It's important that you figure out what these drivers are and include evidence of them in your value proposition statement. Customer value drivers include:

- Key emotional needs

- Ease of use

- Increased revenue

- Faster time to market

- Decreased cost

- Increased profitability

- Improved efficiency

- Increased market share

- Decreased employee turnover

- Reduced customer churn

- Improved customer satisfaction

- Faster turn-around time

One or more of these drivers will most likely affect your target's thinking about what they need to accomplish, and how they are going to get there. Rest assured, there will also be others that are directly related and highly specific to their business needs that do not appear on the list above. You want to be sure to identify the TOP three to five value drivers that your buyers are focused on, to help your value proposition be more relevant and gain their attention.

By now, you should be starting to realize that your value proposition is really telling a story. The more the story is framed from the buyer's point-of-view, as well as their experience and needs, the more likely they will notice and engage with your message and the better they will listen. Many weak value propositions tell the story that the seller wants to tell. The problem lies in the fact that there is no guarantee that it is a story that your targets want to hear. You may end up telling that story to yourself!

So how do we ensure that the story is relevant? Here are four ways to address this:

- **CONNECT** the value proposition of your product or service to three to five of the target's most important decision drivers (review the list of drivers above).

- **COMMUNICATE** how your offer addresses these drivers, in specific terms.

- **QUANTIFY** any driver that you are adding to the story. If you are helping to cut costs, then say by what percentage.

- **DELIVER** proof to back up our statement (testimonials, third-party quotes, references, survey results, case studies, white papers, etc.).

The value proposition story that you tell should "connect the dots" for the buyer, showing them how they will get more in benefits than they will give up in costs. You should be sure to outline both the tangible factors as well as any intangible ones that you know they care about. Make sure that you comprehend what their value drivers are all about. Don't know? ASK THEM! This is not a time for guessing. If you want your value proposition to have teeth, you must put in the work.

And finally, be sure to align your language with how you measure the results of your offer with the buyer. What words do they use to describe their challenges, issues, or goals? How do they measure a successful outcome? Developing the value proposition from an "outside-in" perspective will transform how we tell our product or service story. Here is an example from MediaConvo, Inc. that will help you see how to "translate" language.

Move from "Offer Centric" Language		To "Buyer Centric" Language	
Offer Description	We transform the data into something that clients can take action on.	**Buyer Experience or Situation**	In today's Influence 2.0 world, consumers are creating their own brand dialog by blending your product messaging with their own experiences and opinions, other consumers' input, and traditional media content. Can you afford to be out of sync with your market?
Why They Need It	Look at how wide a net we can cast, and look at how clearly we can identify the key messages and change. Compare that to what it would cost you in traditional market research.	**Our Offer for THAT specific experience or situation**	Our award winning platform, Opus, integrates innovative technology with expert analysis to identify the people, issues and trends impacting your business—at the speed of the market.

Move from "Offer Centric" Language		To "Buyer Centric" Language	
Why it's the Best Offer	Less labor intensive More accurate More on point	**Why This Offer Rather Than Other Options**	We are an innovator in the integration of consumer-generated media and mainstream media, offering access to the greatest breadth of content sources and analytical expertise available in the market.

Standard Pitfalls to Avoid

At this point, you may think that you're almost ready to begin work on your value proposition. You've got great ideas and you're itching to get started. But HOLD ON! I want to be sure that we don't fill up your value proposition with things that hundreds of weak value propositions already use. This is a good time to remember that the goal is to be UNIQUE AND DIFFERENT, which means that we are not going to say the same old things that every one of our competitors are saying. We need to be sure not to use tired, or generic, or unprovable points because we think they sound good, or because our competitor is saying them, and we think we MUST respond by claiming it ourselves. The buyers are looking for a solid reason to buy – and if we and our competitors are all saying similar things, it prolongs the decision process and decreases the likelihood that we get chosen.

Pitfall #1: Don't assume that you know everything about your buyer's goals, motives and needs.

The key word here is "assume." You may think you know everything about their needs, but unless you do the homework to find out directly from a customer or prospect, you are operating on best guess. Typically, when a marketing or a sales person is asked, "What is it that your prospect is trying to achieve here?" the answer is quite often a description of their product or service, or a list of features. The problem is that it doesn't answer the question, which was about the buyer's needs – which may or may not match well with your offering. Understand that the buyer cares more about their needs than they do about the features of your offering. Leading with your product or service doesn't demonstrate any knowledge about the buyer at all. So, if you are assuming you know exactly what will motivate your buyers, be prepared to be wrong. Best guess will maybe get you a 50-50 chance of being right. Gambling with marketing and sales dollars is not a "best practice!"

Pitfall #2: Don't assume that your buyer understands or cares about your goals, motives and efforts.

They don't. It's that simple. They care about themselves first and foremost – which is just human nature. It's all about them, and that's the reality. Therefore, if you make the value proposition all about them, they will pay attention. But if you make it all about your offer, you'll find your assumptions won't take you very far. There's a good chance that it may not even get you an audience with them. The value proposition should demonstrate that you understand and have knowledge about their situation or experience. That is the price of getting their attention. To attract your target buyers, you must talk about them first, to earn the right to add yourself into the equation. Here is the reality: *buyers are always more attracted to themselves and their needs than yours.*

Pitfall #3: Beware of telling them "everything you know."

As marketing and sales people, we tend to want to communicate every single aspect of our offers. We load up brochures, websites, presentations and the like with as much "stuff" as we can. More stuff must equal more value, right? WRONG! Less is more. Don't risk boring the buyer with information they don't need or care about. You don't want to lose their attention because they can't absorb it all. And most importantly, you don't want to make it challenging for them to find out the most important aspects of your offer. Can they find what they need within all that "stuff" that you are communicating? How are they supposed to net it all out to what is only relevant to their needs?

True Story

A few years ago, I participated in developing a client *Content Summit* to kick off a big website rejuvenation project. It was a large technology company and there were 5 different internal groups (50+ people) in the room. Their website at that time had over 5000 pages, and it was as complicated for their buyers to use as it was for them to maintain it. The goal was to simplify it in a big way.

To kick off my work session, I did an exercise that involved locating a particular piece of information on the website. We had five teams who needed to locate some information about a specific customer value driver. We gave them 30 minutes for the exercise.

Result: not one team found content that fit the bill. Not one. They found lots of content, mind you. One team even found a few broken pages! But nothing that was relevant to what we were looking for. Not a terribly impressive buyer experience, to say the least!

Even scarier, each team provided completely different content. There was no overlap from one team to the next. It was hard to figure out what was most relevant, as there were way too many choices. The moral of the story is that if *you* can't easily find the core messages, your prospect won't be able to either. And frankly, they won't try very hard! They will give up quickly if they can't find something relevant, fast.

For this company, who had spent thousands of hours and tens of thousands of dollars on their website, the experience was a real eye-opener. Now, think about your own prospects. Can they find relevant value-based information on your website? Do this exercise with your marketing and sales people and find out for yourself. Be ready to be surprised by what you can't find.

Standard Language to Avoid

The list below outlines descriptors that are included in literally thousands of value propositions. Most of them are not quantified or provable, but companies say them anyway. Why? Because it's easy. Their competitors say them, so there is belief that customers care about them.

Most of these are statements that companies are trumpeting about themselves. They are not objective, and therefore not credible to a prospect or customer. Just because I say that I'm a genius doesn't mean that's a fact! The worst part of these descriptors is that they are not quantified and do not offer objective proof of the statement. Are you using one or more of these now? If so, brace yourself! After each one of these, ask yourself the following question: "According to WHOM?" Unless an objective third party, or existing customer, or industry expert is offering this in specific terms, what you end up with is just "marketing fluff." And fluff just doesn't cut it.

Words That Buyers Won't Buy

- Most Advanced

- Rated best-in-class or "best-of-breed"

- We're Number 1

- We're the "one-stop-shop"

- We offer a full suite of services

- We reduce costs and improve efficiencies

- We're the industry leader

- We are your trusted advisor (or partner)

- We're customer-focused

Now let's think about these items from a prospect or customer point of view.

Your Claim	Your Prospect's Reaction
Most Advanced	How? Can you offer proof of this?
Rated best-in-class or "best-of-breed"	Who rated you that way and what are the specifics of that rating?
We're Number 1	According to whom and by what measurement or metric?
We're the "one-stop-shop"	Is this a top value driver for me? How or why?
We offer a full suite of services	Is that a top value driver for me? How or why?
We reduce costs and improve efficiencies	By how much? Everyone in your market claims this.
We're the industry leader	According to what industry expert?
We're your trusted advisor (or partner)	Does a formal relationship exist, or is this just wishful thinking?
We're customer-focused	How? Can you quantify that? Proof?

If you honestly think that some of these standard descriptors are important to your prospect or customer, then you need to be certain that you deliver them in a specific and measurable way. They must be relevant, and not sound like a "me too" statement that everyone in your market is also claiming. It's about being "different," not the same as everyone else.

Here are some final thoughts before we start crafting our value proposition.

1   **Beware of making it all about your product or service.** It isn't really about your company or your product or your service. Ask your prospects and they will tell you it better be all about them. Otherwise, they are not going to spend much time considering your offer, or they may not to talk to you at all.

2   **Beware of making generic statements.** Back it up or back it out of your value proposition. Generic doesn't sell, and it isn't believable.

3   **Beware of using one value proposition for all customer segments and industries.** One-size-fits-all never really fits anyone. So be ready to have some tailored, specific value propositions for different vertical industries, and different customer segments, personas, or titles. Develop one core value proposition, then map out the variations you'll need.

4   **Beware of not offering proof.** If you can't prove it, it's not going to have any impact on the prospect. They'll know you can't prove it, and that makes you look weak!

5   **Beware of sounding too complicated.** If it isn't readily understood, you'll lose people quickly. Prospects have neither the time nor the desire to figure it out. Make it simple and clear.

6 **Beware of using too much industry lingo.** We assume that they will "get it," but what if that is an incorrect assumption? If you must use lingo, be sure to explain it. And if it's internal lingo that only your company uses, get it out of there! It's not relevant or understandable to your audience. No one is impressed with it, and it comes off as sloppy!

Be prepared to go through several drafts of each of the pieces of your **Value Proposition Platform**. It takes thought, input from other key people in your organization, external input, research, and refinement. Whether you are in a small company or a large one, there are choices to be made about who to include in the development process. Input from the following areas will be helpful:

- Marketing

- Product Development

- Sales

- Public Relations

- Analyst Relations

- Customers (new, happy, and former)

- Partners

- Market Analysts

Each of these functional areas can provide valuable input into the design and development process to help you hone a strong, differentiated value proposition. It is also important that you have all the other pieces we include in the platform to support the statement.

When you have additional staff available to participate in the design process, you can assign different sections to individuals or teams. For the main value proposition statements, make sure that all your team members participate in the development. Group input here is invaluable in fleshing out the strongest value proposition. I'd suggest a series of brain storming sessions (2-3) to get a rough draft developed. Marketing will take care of the refinement.

Do not fail to get Sales input, because at the end of the day, they will be most engaged in using the value proposition in prospect and customer conversations. The value proposition statement can be extended into an elevator speech, a tag line, embedded in sales presentations, and built into sales scripts, sales prompters and tools that sales people can use during the sales process. If you don't get input from Sales up front, and then the value proposition doesn't work well for them right away, you can be sure that they won't use it and will make up what they need on their own. This will provide inconsistent brand messaging across your sales force, and cause confusion and lack of clarity with your target offer.

Building a Value Proposition Platform for Buyers

Designing a cadence of value proposition messages that move with the buyer through their journey is the best way to ensure that the right combination of value and insights is served up when buyers (and your sellers) need it most. In working with B2B marketing and sales teams over the years, I have developed a platform approach to value propositions that can map to the buyer journey in the manner that buyers prefer to be communicated with. This requires a modular approach to building a value proposition. Using only a short elevator speech misses the point of what buyers really need as they progress towards a decision.

Perhaps one of the reasons that buyers have commandeered the sales process is because they cannot rely on vendors to deliver relevance across the range of information that they provide. It all starts with the value proposition, which gives the first real indicator of whether we are tuned in and communicating in a way that resonates with their reality. Given that most value propositions have inherent weaknesses, you can clearly shine a light on differentiation by crafting your value proposition with a platform approach.

Important Considerations and Factors

- Move to buyer relevant, customer focused descriptions and language, rather than a feature-focused approach.

- Make every effort to tailor and personalize by highly segmented targets to enable you to drive relevant conversations.

- Get out there early and deliver your message to buyers before, during, and after engagement with your sales people.

- Consider more thought leadership style content, rather than just promotional or transactional content, as it allows you to serve up insight-driven value proposition messaging.

- Finally, Product Development and Management need to evolve to help Product Marketing move off the old feature / function orientation, and work to align the value proposition to the buyer at every stage to drive *relevance* – the one major thing that all buyers are looking for.

VALUE POINTS

The Value Proposition Platform includes the Audience Definition and the 3-part Value Proposition Statement for a specific value prop. You may need different versions of your value proposition for industry segments, product or service lines, or even to customize for specific buyers.

Make sure to include up to 3 key value drivers, quantify them, and offer proof. It sets your sales people up for success when using the value prop in both digital and live conversations.

Beware of the standard pitfalls and avoid including untested assumptions about your buyer. Do some buyer research and make sure you understand their key business needs.

Ironically, almost all companies use a short list of the same standard words and phrases to differentiate themselves! Be more original and relevant than that.

Get a team on board to help draft a value proposition, you need their perspective and buy-in. Think Product, Marketing, Sales. Run the final draft by customers to make sure you nailed it!

4

Conducting Essential Research

FROM THE RESEARCH:
PAY ATTENTION TO BUYER JOURNEY STAGES!

We asked respondents which value proposition area was the most important at each buying stage. The buying stages were defined as follows:

General Education	(Awareness)
Business Case	(Consideration)
Implementation Scenario/Evaluation	(Consideration)
Short List	(Preference)
Final Decision	(Purchase)

From the seller's point of view, the most critical stages are being added to the short list and making the final decision. While there are variations in the importance of value proposition areas across the buying stages, three areas were important at every stage and grew in importance during the last two buying stages:

Most important	"Impact on Our Organization"
Second	"Relevance to a Specific Need"
Third	"Tangible Business Benefits"

According to our respondents, these three areas of importance represented 47% of the General Education/Awareness stage but 59% of the Final Decision / Purchase stage.

As this data indicates, **understanding** that your value proposition must be relevant to your buyers' needs is a long way from actually **creating** a value proposition that fulfills all of the needs of all the buyers throughout all stages of their buying journey. Many variables come into play at different stages, and your sales team needs to be equipped with information about how it all works and what messages belong in the playbook at each stage. We need to gather information on all the key areas of importance, paying special attention to the three most important, as listed above.

Before we start to put any words into the mouths of your sellers, we need to do three pieces of research.

1   We need to hear the buyer's point-of-view, their words right out of their own mouths.

2   We need to do a study of the value proposition language that your most important competitors are using, so that we won't fall into the trap of copycat language or industry jargon.

3 We need to do some internal research. It's a good idea to learn what people in your own organization think your value proposition is right now. Meet with Marketing, Sales, Customer Service, and Product Management. It will surely be enlightening! The combination of external and internal research will provide a solid foundation as we begin developing our value proposition.

Interview Your Organization's Top Sales People

Hold a round table discussion with sales leaders to get their "selling" language and perspectives on the table. Some of the questions to be considered during conversations with our sales experts include the following:

- What do buyers and customers say they need when they are talking about our products or services?

- What do buyers and customers say they do NOT need?

- What matters to our buyers and customers when they are considering our type of offering?

- What are the words and phrases that they use to describe their business issues and problem symptoms?

- How do they describe the outcomes or solutions that they are seeking?

- What specifically about our product or service offerings do they like?

- What do they want more of versus areas where they feel improvements are needed?

- What is missing from our product or service offering?

- Are there any areas where you think the company falls short?

- Where do they seem to prefer our competitors?

- What do they give us high marks for?

- What do they simply put up with because they can't get anything better?

- How deep do you feel our existing customer's loyalty to be?

- How do customers describe or define our products and services, and what words do they use?

- What are they waiting for us to change or improve?

This conversation will give you a great start and get your sales team involved in the process.

Download Sales Questions   http://www.valueproposition.expert/salesquestions

---

Mining Customer Service and Support

Do the same thing with a few key agents from Customer Service and Support, both inside and field support people, if you have them. Service personnel often have first-hand details regarding the customer experience that sales does not. This can uncover common challenges customers may be having, product or service misconceptions or issues, and much more. Oftentimes, Customer Service is overlooked for this kind of research because there is a misconception that it may all be about bad news. Quite the contrary! This could be a gold mine of customer information. Ask for trouble tickets or chat room dialogs that reveal language that customers use when describing our products and services. How do they describe their difficulties, and what kind of changes do the service agents make for them? This will help us get closer and closer into the lives of customers who are actually interacting with our products or services daily. Use the same interview questions listed above for sales, as many of them will also be relevant for conversations with Customer Service personnel, as well.

Conduct Focus Groups with Customers

If it's in the budget, focus groups are an excellent way to get at the business issues that are on your customers' minds. It's not always a *problem*, you know. Sure, they may be seeking to solve a problem, but maybe they come to you to gain advantages of speed, or product innovation, or fantastic customer service. A focus group allows you to listen in as they discuss their business issues. The interactions that focus group members have with each other can also uncover a lot of very important and relevant attitudes, understandings, misconceptions, competitive insights, desires, needs, and language that will be extremely helpful as you begin to construct the value proposition "story."

Survey or Interview Key Customer Groups (New, Happy, and Former)

As an alternative to a focus group, we can survey or do telephone interviews of our customers. It is most helpful to do this with a mix of brand new customers, happy current customers, and former customers. This will yield a range of priceless information in the buyers' own language. Understanding why a new customer just decided in our favor can give key insights into the actual buying decision while it is still fresh. Understanding what makes longer-term customers happy is also crucial information to gather. And finally, to achieve a 360-degree view of our customers experience and thoughts, it can be extremely revealing to get input from customers who have stopped doing business with us and moved on to competitors or to an internal solution. Why did they leave? What was the compelling event? How did a competitor convince them to move to a different option? Be sure to sample people from each of the decision-maker titles as well as a couple of key influencer titles. The following is a list of the questions to be used with each specific group:

New Customer Interview Questions

- Can you share with me why you were considering a new vendor in this area? What needs or challenges were you focused on?

- What were the main drivers of your decision to select [YOUR COMPANY NAME]?

- How did they compare with the other companies you considered?

- What was the most important factor for you that made them your choice?

- In your opinion, what truly differentiated [YOUR COMPANY NAME] from the other vendors you considered?

- How did you become acquainted with [YOUR COMPANY NAME]?

- If it was a referral, from whom did it come, and how did the experience ultimately compare to what the referral party shared with you about [YOUR COMPANY NAME]?

Current Customer Interview Questions

- What do you feel are the main areas of value provided by your relationship with [YOUR COMPANY NAME] to support your needs?

- What are the core reasons that your partnership with them works for your organization?

- Can you share with me what you think their value proposition is from your point of view?

- If someone you knew was looking for a vendor to provide [PRODUCT OR SERVICE AREA] – would you recommend [YOUR COMPANY NAME]? If yes, why? If no, why not?

- What should other companies who may be looking for a vendor to provide [PRODUCT OR SERVICE AREA] absolutely know about [YOUR COMPANY NAME] during the decision process?

- In your opinion, what differentiates [YOUR COMPANY NAME] from other similar vendors out there?

Former Custmer Interview Questions:

- How long did you work with [YOUR COMPANY NAME]? What value did they bring to your organization during that time?

- Given that you made a choice to move to a different vendor, what changed in your thinking or experience that made you switch?

- What are the most important drivers of value to you in working with a vendor who provides [PRODUCT OR SERVICE AREA]?

- Can you share with me what you believe your current provider's value proposition is for your organization?

- What makes them different or stand out from [YOUR COMPANY NAME] in your opinion?

- What would have made the difference for you to consider keeping [YOUR COMPANY NAME] as your vendor?

Download Customer Questions	http://www.valueproposition.expert/customerquestions

Live Examples of Research

A good first step is to conduct face-to-face or telephone interviews with members of the executive team, to find out how they perceive elements of the current value proposition. The following table outlines the key points raised in interviews with MediaConvo company personnel as part of the value proposition project. Nine people were interviewed. To highlight the conversations, key comments were sorted into categories which may help identify patterns or highlight some of the interesting ideas and thoughts that were shared.

Internal Interviews

Key Executives from MediaConvo, Inc.

1 Why do you think customers choose MediaConvo over the alternatives?

People	Customer service
	Relationship with sales person
	High-touch support
	We'll do anything we have to do to have a successful implementation – to make sure we've satisfied the customer
	Client relationship – from implementation to launch to ongoing support – our relationship with the customer doesn't end
Technology	Natural language technology
	Technology coupled with consulting practice
	We can still talk about this because our biggest competitors don't talk much about this
Services	Converging both Mainstream Media (MSM) and Consumer-Generated Media (CGM)
	Consulting services around technology to interpret the data
	Full spectrum of services – automation & analysis, best of both worlds
	Enterprise-wide measurement
	Reporting, automated analysis, one-stop-shopping
	Voice of the consumer- where is that voice? Our job is to know where it is and to go there
	Newer clients are choosing us because of the CGM capabilities
	Pitch pure Public Relations (PR) measurement for those who just want that, or we can do both

Method	Holistic approach: tool, reporting, expertise, advisors
	Accuracy, precision
	Better at collecting, managing and correlating data – and delivering it any way that you need it
	The sophistication of our tools and to be able to manage large amounts of information – for large companies – companies who need to do deeper analytics
Outcomes	Cents into dollar signs as raw content is spun into relevant content
	Moving from anecdotal evidence or lone voice to the aggregated voice of trends and patterns
	Crossover – helping Public Relations teams to be tactical AND strategic – as well as providing Marketing with strategic information as well

2 What do you think the MediaConvo's value proposition is?

Our Offer	Convergence of CGM/MSM (first to market)
	Part content. Part tool/utility
	Accuracy
	Keeping track of your company's brands
	Proving your worth as PR (team or individual professional)
	Tracking campaign impact and fixing/changing it as it rolls out
	Individual needs in PR group or Marketing group – presenting the data and analyzing the data to present it internally
	Talk to the people who are passionate about your product (positively or negatively)
	The tool isn't the whole thing anymore – it's really about the output and the analysis – we've become more of a consultant – and this is the right direction. It's hard to show the value of a tool to someone who is really busy!
Outcomes	Giving clients ideas on what the data means and giving them ideas on how to use it
	Transforming the data into something that clients can act on
Method	Looking at things through the eyes of a marketer
	Less labor intensive
	More accurate
	More on-point
	Haven't built a human brain yet!! So, technology is an enabler – but the human element is key
	Comparative play: Look at how wide a net we can cast, and look at how clearly we can identify the key messages and change. Compare that to what it would cost you in traditional market research.

3   Does any of the competitor's messaging resonate for you, and if so, why?

Unspecified competitors	Focused on education
	Identifies the fear/pain
	Everyone is trying to define themselves – it all sounds the same
	Deployment time is faster than us.
	Hard to justify our offer/price with other alternatives
Competitor A	Being advanced in understanding of CGM – leadership role
	Chief Marketing Officer – as industry leader
Competitor B	Ability to tie CGM to demographics
Competitor C	Do good great job of case studies and showing what they can do - can always illustrate what they are doing.
	Do a good job of focusing on the verticals and showcasing what they actually can do in each vertical
	They can show a report on each vertical that clearly illustrates it. We still talk in generalities in this area
Competitor D	Price is pretty competitive though they don't deliver the quality we do
	Did a really good job with defining what automated Public Relations measurement was – helped us in our branding at that time
	Saw a presentation by at the Public Relations Society of America (PRSA) show – and they were showing their own results from their product – without pitching them – and I came away from that saying, "I need that stuff!"

4 In getting MediaConvo's message out there – what do you think customers/prospects REALLY need to know?

About Customers	Lead with topical focus on customer issues, not with MediaConvo's capabilities
	Simple language, customer voice, all levels in the target company needs to be able to understand it
	50/50 desire or need to have online access versus just getting the analysis and reports
About MediaConvo	We understand the function (PR & Marketing)
	We understand the industries we are in (Pharma, Financial Services, etc.)
	We are not just a software provider – we need to show we can extend the relationship
	We're leader in this space
	Most accurate, precise, up-do-date and real-time solution for analysis, discovery and reporting of trends from all types of media
	To get result,s you need trends, analysis, segmentation, thought process
	What are we? Market research company, technology company, technology-enabled marketing services company – we don't seem to have decided
	We have a hard time showing results of what customers are getting
	On CGM side, sometimes unclear to customers how MUCH content they are going to get
	Misunderstandings on who pays for traditional content – and that customers have to license that separately

5   What has been missing from MediaConvo's external communications that we should consider now?

Customers	People want advice on how to run their business – actionable intelligence
	Don't know how far we'll go to make sure they are happy
	Customer service – how much we give
	Do customers know that we're a leader in CGM?
Technology	Technology as an up-sell of services – i.e. Marketing doesn't have time to do it for themselves, rather than the reverse
Services	Talk about services more clearly – not just technology
	What is our product versus our services? Not always clear what the direction is?
Method	Analysis of the data is really important – either you do it, or we do it
	We can give the answers – not just the data
	Best of technology, best of human analysis for contextual accuracy
	Automation & human analysis
Outcomes	What are the outputs that a customer is going to get? - Reports
	What are you going to do with the information?
	How are you going to use it?

6 What do prospects/customers not understand about our offers that we need to be sure to cover?

Customers	The time investment on customers' part to customize our program dashboard up front
	The questions we can answer
	How will our services help them? Department, individual role?
	Competitive advantage – information growing out of control
Technology	The time involved in utilizing the software (deployment and usage)
	Look at the solution – not just the technology
Services	Understanding what to track with CGM
	How flexible we are – and how we handle changes
Method	We're not a content partner
	Our solution is a combination of content, tool, reports
	The need to apply human intellect – and how we do this. Often transparent to the client that we do this (customers are really more into the output/report than the process we took to get there)
Outcomes	That the data isn't the entire thing – analysis is the true outcome

Internal Research Summary

A clear theme across the interviews was the need for a shift away from the focus on being a "technology company." The primary targets are Marketing and Public Relations, who are not as focused on the technology itself. They are interested in the outputs to help them make sense of both mainstream and consumer-generated media. So, selling a "technology" is not the best message for this audience. There seems to be a lack of clarity on what the final strategic direction is or should be – Marketing Services versus Marketing Research, versus some other undefined category. There is a strong desire for simpler, more customer-focused messaging, and a clear, short and distinct answer to "What does MediaConvo do?" An important take-away is the idea that the focus needs to be technology AND human analysis, as well as service, consulting, and interpretation. It seemed clear that it was necessary to add that piece of the puzzle that customers ultimately need when dealing with customer-generated media (CGM) and mainstream media (MSM) data. This research sends a clear message to MediaConvo's marketing team that brand messaging is currently missing the mark with their two primary audiences. However, the research project already uncovers specific sources of confusion and suggests potential remedies.

Notice that this is a common occurrence in product companies, especially technology companies. Over time, you develop an extended suite of services around your product or products. If your value proposition doesn't evolve with the addition and evolution of your services, you'll find an increasing challenge in effectively getting your message across to prospects. The value proposition story becomes unclear or inconsistent, or missing key elements, making it difficult for your sellers and your buyers to truly understand your combined offering.

External Research: Customers of MediaConvo, Inc.

The following statements were taken from a review of MediaConvo's customer testimonials, as well as a scan of any available testimonials on competitor websites. It's often helpful to see how, and in what words, customers are describing their experience. We supplemented this with actual interviews, but doing a testimonial scan is a great way to prepare for a live conversation and formulate the right questions. These statements are a combination of descriptions of customer experiences with MediaConvo, Inc., as well as with competing companies.

- Helps us to assess how well we are conveying our message.

- Gives us a true sense of our impact in the market place.

- Provides us with the means not only to measure blogs but also to track our messages and see the content.

- Uncovering trends and relationships that are meaningful to our business.

- Measure our mentions and key message pickup to assist in providing valid data to management about the success of our media relations efforts relative to competitors.

- Dynamically adjust campaigns based on what is happening now – not what happened three months ago.

- [The software] is a strategic tool, a tactical tool and an information management system.

- It's an element used in near real time to drive what we call rapid response.

- Provide the measurement, strategic assessment and reporting tools all marketing professionals need, designed for the way they work.

- MediaConvo is smart to give its customers equal access to what all of us out there are saying, not just the anointed few in the press.

- Helps us to identify, track and listen to the online influencers as a first line of contact with consumers.

- The ability to quickly, easily and accurately monitor attitudes and opinions provided by [competitor company] is critical information when evaluating a company's reputation in the market.

- Provides a new way of putting information into context.

- MediaConvo is clearly among that group of companies offering innovative market intelligence solutions that allow its clients to accurately measure and analyze media coverage, market leadership, and corporate reputation in real-time.

- Because blogs both break news stories and add additional context and thoughtful discussion to stories from more traditional media sources, monitoring their output is essential to successful marketing efforts.

- A solid way to measure and evaluate its brand positioning. It also is a way to uncover media trends.

- It's not always quantity; it's quality of coverage that's important. It's nice to have something that depicts both. (Note: quantity or quality? What if you could have both?)

- Out maneuver competitors when it has mattered most, reversing negative trends, improving customer support for targeted products, and dramatically improving its reputation and brand equity as indicated by independent surveys.

- Understanding marketplace perception.

- Enhance our corporate reputation using our strengths and our competitors' weaknesses.

- Competing globally for media mindshare.

- Increase positive coverage to help drive sales.

- Centralize content and performance metrics.

- Grasp customer needs as they are being expressed.

- Teach your brands some new tricks.

- Target your audience intelligently.

- Beware of the influence of the lowly consumer.

- Brand message research.

As you watch the MediaConvo value proposition unfold and observe multiple versions of some of its components, look for the influence of some of the research that we conducted before even beginning to write. It is strongly advisable to follow a similar path with your own research before you start writing.

There's another type of external research that is hugely important: a competitive messaging scan which is about assessing and comparing competitors' value propositions as well as related brand and positioning statements in relation to your own. That's the only way you can ensure that your language is original and differentiated! Use a messaging scan template for collecting this information by scouring competitor's websites, professional literature, analyst reports, and customer testimonials.

Use this template to gather messaging information. It will tell you what to look for and serve as a sample template for reporting your results. The numbered slots indicate places to add your own topics that may be of particular interest to your target audience. Below the sample, you will find a few examples of the scan I did for MediaConvo, Inc.

FACTORS	Your Company	Competitor 1	Competitor 2	Competitor 3	Competitor 4
Focus					
Tagline					
Keywords					
Value Proposition "What we do"					
Positioning Focus					
Differentiators					
Brand Questions					
Customer Targets					
Offerings					

Download Competitor Messaging Scan   http://www.valueproposition.expert/competitormessagescan

External Research:
Competitive Messaging Analysis for MediaConvo, Inc.

Focus

MediaConvo	Competitors				
CGM & MSM	CGM & MSM	CGM & MSM	CGM only	CGM Only	MSM only

(CGM = Consumer-Generated Media, MSM = Mainstream Media)

Taglines

MediaConvo	Reputation Intelligence
	Better Decisions. Faster
Competitors	The Leader in Market Intelligence
	The new global measurement standard in consumer-generated media
	A Market Intelligence Revolution
	Fearlessly seeking the reasons why
	To a marketer or manufacturer this is noise. To us, it's the sound of consumer experience.
	Powerful technology with human intelligence to deliver actionable brand protection and market intelligence solutions that solve everyday business problems
	Manage Risk. Leverage Opportunity
	Insight Expertise Strategy

Value Propositions

Competitors	Reputation Intelligence enables you to understand how perceptions found in the media and public opinion affect your company's bottom line, so you can formulate proactive reputation and brand-management strategies.
	Helps businesses and government organizations succeed by providing market intelligence that delivers a 360-degree view of your company, your competitors, and your market. We deliver real-time insight you can use to be more strategic, more competitive, and ultimately more profitable.
	A market intelligence company that tracks, analyzes and distills consumer opinions and perceptions of the online world – consisting of more than 27 million blogs, message boards, opinion sites, and other public forums –into insights about companies, products, people, and issues.
	Able to "see" the "peaks of passion" in online conversations to understand customer motivations. We use a combination of proprietary software and world-class analysts to explore what drives customer behavior. Think of it as a quantitative research with the richness of qualitative data, but more honest and faster than both.
	Deciphers valuable business intelligence from the noise of people's own online words, using an unequalled pairing of online dialogue management expertise and proprietary technology.

Differentiators

MediaConvo Before	Competitors			
Best service in the industry – 90% client renewal	Point of view sentiment – tone measurement	Defining business and marketing intelligence space	Impartiality of our role as listener	8 years of experience mining and facilitating online discussion
First to market with CGM/MSM Solution	Applying marketing intelligence to business problems	Technology leadership: federated content discovery	Putting the power of information in your hands and not forcing you to engage in long-term consulting assignments	
Thought leaders in CGM applications	Extensive backgrounds in business intelligence and analytics solutions	Content mining	The principals have over 30 years of combined expertise and experience in developing marketing intelligence applications using natural language processing and machine learning	
Best overall accuracy: best technology paired with human analysis		ROI driven solutions		
Tracks interplay between MSM and CGM		Unique methodologies		
		Analysts		
		Leader in Word-of-Mouth (WOM) marketing		

To recap, we have internal interviews, external testimonials, customer questions, and a competitive messaging scan. This provides a great deal of solid information to use as we begin to build our value proposition. It's not *everything* that we need, but it's a lot! The final type of external research needed is plain old market research on your target market(s). If that hasn't been updated recently, now's the perfect time to do so.

Overall, when it comes to building a buyer-focused value proposition, never start with a blank piece of paper. This will result in an "inside-out" value proposition, which has a very low likelihood of resonating with an "outside" prospect.

Extended Example: Top Line Sales

Top Line Sales is a service business. The president, Lisa Magnuson, is a solopreneur who has built a successful company. Our value proposition approach was a little bit different, as she did not have internal stakeholders to consult for the initial research phase. She worked with me, of course, and also sought input from a mastermind group of business owners of which she is a member. They provided a valuable sounding board for her.

Top Line Sales offers a totally different perspective on how to know your customers and your market. Here are some ways in which Lisa's market differed from MediaConvo's:

- Lisa was in a stable niche market; MediaConvo was in a highly competitive, highly disruptive, fast-moving new market with new players every day.

- Top Line Sales' market was well-known to Lisa. She formerly worked inside many of the companies to whom she now sells, in the same capacity to which she now sells. Therefore, she understood her target individuals very well.

- Lisa needs just a handful of new prospects, because 100% of her clients are referrals; on the other hand, MediaConvo needed hundreds of new, unknown clients in multiple industries.

In fact, Lisa knew her clients intimately. She hosted mastermind groups of 6-8 regional sales vice presidents, who paid her to lead the group. Through that regular contact about their key business issues, she was constantly informed about their needs, their interests, and the issues that are relevant to them. As such, she had no need to conduct additional research to learn about her customers. But to be sure, Lisa habitually conducts "retrospective" interviews at the conclusion of client engagements, and whenever a proposal or bid is awarded elsewhere. So, she stays up to date on former clients, as well as reasons that prospects or previous customers chose a competitive business.

Given all of that, one might ask, why did Lisa need a value proposition at all?

Here's why. This is what she wanted for Top Line Sales.

- Her business had hit a plateau. Her deals were on the small side, revenue was unpredictable, and she had too many long-term coaching clients paying lower fees in a program that she no longer wanted to continue. Essentially, she had outgrown her original business model and wanted to take it to the next level.

- She wanted to earn much more money by working more strategically, not just working more hours. Lisa had developed hundreds of training tools, but they didn't really "add up" to a set of processes or a system that would lead to bigger, longer term, more strategic engagements. It was hard to tell what the real "offer" was. There were too many options!

- Although referrals are great, Lisa wanted to be able to bring in business more predictably. For that she needed more of a social media presence, more visible thought leadership, a compelling value proposition and better messaging in all regards that clearly communicated the value her company delivered.

Top Line Sales Market and Customer Knowledge

Given that the company already had access to a lot of external customer research, our approach was to zero in first on her core target markets, so we could significantly narrow the focus to develop a highly differentiated message.

Top Line Sales (TLS) – Audience Definition:

- **B2B COMPANIES** that have the proper products or services to sell 7-figure deals into their prospect accounts.

- **ANNUAL REVENUE**: $10 million and above. Companies with one or more sales people on their team. The financial foundation and ability to pay TLS fees to help them land TOP Line Accounts™. Fortune 500 companies that see the value of this approach and need additional resources to achieve it.

- **TARGET CONTACT**: Vice President of Sales or Vice President of Sales and Marketing, Director of Sales, CEO, Business Owner

- **CONTACT PRIORITIES**: Interested in the TLS niche – landing TOP Line Accounts™ (including new, retention and expansion of existing accounts), wants to augment current efforts and resources, desire to put a methodology in place to land large deals.

- **MEDIUM TO LONG SALES CYCLE** (Larger sales opportunities, not a commodity sale.)

- **REFERRAL**: Best success rate is a referral. (Note: *Every* current existing client of TLS is from a referral.)

Here is the Top Line Sales response to its own questions in the competitor assessment grid. Unlike MediaConvo, Inc., Top Line Sales doesn't have a competitor problem, nor does it have as much of a differentiation problem, either. Rather, it has the challenge of changing the nature of its value proposition to customers who already see value but need to experience it at a much higher and more strategic way within their companies.

Factors	Company: Top Line Sales
Focus	Top Line Accounts
Tagline	Seven-figure contracts
Keywords	War room
	"roll up our sleeves. Not just "advice-givers"
	Live deal coaching
	Field-proven
Positioning Focus	Information Technology companies
Differentiators	Coaching a large account sales team throughout a long-term 7-figure account deal (12-18 months) until they win
	"win themes"
	100% referral business

Factors	Company: Top Line Sales
Customer Targets	Vice President of Sales whose: • Sales people know how to identify large opportunities • Basic sales training and practices in place • Sales people have minimum of five years' experience • No or little strategic sales training or programs in place • Existing national/global account programs in place (we can augment/enhance) • Non-salespeople involved with top customers (Beyond Customer Service - sales workshops) • Also, owners/CEOs in the same types of companies.
Customer Challenges	Sales people are primarily consumed with small, immediate transactions and related firefighting, allowing Top Line Account™ development to fall by the wayside. Therefore, these large contracts are either missed or lost. Sales VPs are stretched too thin to consistently focus on strategic account development, leaving sellers without the expertise and coaching needed to develop, close and/or retain BIG deals. Therefore, millions of dollars of revenue potential can be left on the table. Most companies lack an ingrained and disciplined formula to unlock the winning code for landing TOP Line Accounts™, creating unpredictable and inconsistent results, thereby losing the multiplier effect associated with accumulating marquee accounts.

Many companies that hire Top Line Sales have typically hired a sales training or management consulting company to try and upgrade their sales results. Very few companies do precisely what TLS does, directed specifically at the Sales Vice President or Sales Manager, and working with the sales team and the sales team leader together on large deals. It is a very hands-on offering, rather than typical training. It is highly skilled work that requires a great deal of industry experience.

Given that, does TLS actually have competition? Of course. But it is very indirect. When Lisa gets in front of a prospect, it's not hard to differentiate herself from any sales trainer. Few consulting firms do such specific, hands-on engagements with sales leaders the way TLS does.

If your company doesn't fall into this kind of category, do not worry. You will have different challenges in other sections of your value proposition. Every organization has its own market challenges. The **Value Proposition Platform** approach can address all types.

VALUE POINTS

First-hand qualitative research with internal and external stakeholders is crucial to preparing the creation of a buyer-focused value proposition.

Interview internal key executives to learn the current gaps in your own company's understanding of the existing value proposition.

Roundtables with the Sales team and Customer Service agents will provide insights on how your customers talk about your company and products.

Talk to three groups of buyers: newly won customers, current happy customers, and former customers. Make sure to include both decision makers and influencers as they both participate in the buyer journey.

Update your general market research for every market that you sell into. Understanding what is driving the markets of your buyers helps you understand what decisions they need to make, and why.

If you know your customers and market in different ways, use the knowledge that you have. Just be certain that it's authentic. Then supplement it to cover gaps or new areas. Be wary of relying on assumptions. You could be wrong!

5

Identifying Your Target Audience

FROM THE RESEARCH: KNOW YOUR BUYERS!

Here's what we know about the buyers in our research study. Knowing their characteristics may help you gauge their responses in terms of your own audience. While this research focused on technology buyers, note the decision-making team make-up. Your own offering will have similarities. Few B2B buying decisions are made alone.

Role in the purchase decision process: (68% high-level decision-makers)

Technical Decision Maker	25%
Business Decision Maker	24%
Executive Decision Maker	18%
Financial Decision Maker	11%

Internal Consultant	11%
Technical Evaluator/Recommender	8%
Independent Consultant	2%

Primary Focus in Making Purchase Decisions:

Technical Impact	47%
Business Impact	34%
Financial Impact	19%

Decision-Making Style:

Collaborator	40%
Challenger	34%
Advocate	26%

Participants were asked whether their greatest area of focus through the buying process was outcomes, processes, or people:

#1 Focus on Outcomes	47%
#1 Focus on Processes	27%
#1 Focus on People	24%

When you participate in a purchase decision as part of a buying team which of the following phrases best describes your approach?

Work as a Team & Weigh all Pros, Cons and Opinions	42%
Challenge Thoughts, Solutions & Viewpoints to Make Best Choice	30%
Make Things Happen and Take the Best Action	28%

Knowing is the Path to Relevance

If relevance to the buyer is the most critical element in a value proposition, we need to deeply know and understand the buyers. The buyers told us that, didn't they? They said only two-thirds of value propositions were at all relevant, and at best the range of relevance they experienced topped at 71% with the lowest at 30% relevant! As both marketers and sellers, we have tremendous room for improvement here. Where else in terms of strategy or tactics can we find that *scope of opportunity* to gain an extraordinary advantage in the buying process? The key to differentiation resides squarely in our ability to be as relevant to the buyer's experience, needs, wants, challenges or objectives as we can. This differentiates you by default, as most of the competition will be too busy talking about their own company and their own products and services, to the exclusion of their buyers. Think about it. That could be where you are right now with your own value proposition, right?

But if your company wants to make relevance the focus of your value messaging, you will have to dig very deep into learning about your buyers. You may think you already do, but are you sure you really know the market dynamics that are impacting their business – from their point of view?

Start from the beginning: Who Are Your Targets?

The brief review of the buyer demographics cited at the beginning of this chapter should give us all pause. All these buyers, or people like them in other purchase scenarios, will make up the group of buyers for any big sale from your company. The research confirmed that they will demand relevance to their business issues. While there are themes and possible similarities across different industries and buyers, you and your team must discover exactly what YOUR buyers' specific business issues are. Uncovering this foundational perspective will go a long way to helping you to explain your products and services in such a way that resonates with the buyers.

Let's clarify everything that you'll need to learn about the buyers before you begin to construct your value proposition:

- Your primary **industry sector** and **segments**. If you serve multiple industries, you may need multiple versions of your value proposition.

- **Titles** of decision-makers (actual buyers) and influencers (individuals whose approval the buyers depend on before saying yes to you).

- **Business issues** of concern to both the buyers and influencers.

Segmenting your market

We need to divide our broad targeted market into just those who have a common set of needs, priorities, and goals that we can address with our product or service. Identification of targeted sectors or industry or sub-industries is an important step in setting the stage for developing the value proposition. What are your primary sectors and industries? What segments within them do you target? Another way of looking at this is to ask, "Where are we going to aim our marketing and sales efforts?" We want to identify the best-fit targets that will be receptive and have a need for your offerings.

Here are key criteria for defining a market segment:

- It is measurable.

- It has enough breadth to be profitable.

- It is a stable segment that has longevity.

- It is reachable through your marketing and sales efforts.

- It will respond consistently with the right marketing approach.

- It is reachable in a cost-effective manner.

- You can get supporting data about the segment for market positioning and sales approaches.

Selecting Sectors, Industries and Segments

A good source to begin with is the North American Industry Classification System or NAICS. This system codifies businesses according the type of economic activities they engage in. It covers the United States, Canada and Mexico. It replaced the well-known SIC codes (*Standard Industrial Classification* system) back in 1997. While SIC codes are still being used by the U.S. Security and Exchange Commission, the NAICS codes are more up to date relative to businesses today. It may not cover newer or emerging markets, but it is a strong start to refining your targets.

Before you start to build out your target audience, it is important to understand two of the building blocks: sectors and industries. Frequently these are used interchangeably, but there are some differences to note.

- A **SECTOR** is a classification that covers a broad base of companies within the economy. Think of it as the first level of breaking down your market into industries, and sub-industries.

- An **INDUSTRY** is the next level and is a more specific group of companies that share a similar set of business activities.

NAICS provides 20 sectors with all the industry breakdowns at www.NAICS.com. It is a credible source for evaluating and selecting the foundation for your target audience. An added benefit is that NAICS can also be very helpful in building or enhancing marketing and sales lists for promotional and sales activities. There are many other more sophisticated sources of contact data, but this is a good place to start to think about, or revisit, building or augmenting your lists.

The following table provides a sample breakdown of key sectors, and the industries each sector represents. For the purposes of your **Value Proposition Platform** pick a primary sector and industry as a foundational approach. You may play in multiple sectors and industries – and the value proposition may be quite different or have significant differences in those other areas. Simply repeat the **Value Proposition Platform** process if you want to focus on additional sectors/industries. You may find it only necessary to change sections of it, or you may need to construct a new one to address very specific needs of your additional industry.

Sectors	Industries
Consumer Discretionary	Auto Components
	Automobiles
	Distributors
	Diversified Consumer Services
	Electronics
	Hotels, Restaurants & Leisure
	Household Durables
	Internet & Catalog Retail
	Leisure Products
	Media
	Multiline Retail
	Specialty Retail
	Textiles, Apparel & Luxury Goods

Sectors	Industries
Consumer Staples	Beverages
	Food & Staples Retailing
	Food Products
	Household Products
	Personal Products
	Tobacco
Energy	Energy Equipment & Services
	Fuels
Financial	Banks
	Capital Markets
	Consumer Finance
	Diversified Financial Services
	Insurance
	Real Estate Investment Trusts
	Real Estate Management & Development
	Thrifts & Mortgage Finance
Health Care	Biotechnology
	Healthcare Equipment & Supplies
	Healthcare Technology
	Life Sciences Tools & Services
	Pharmaceuticals

Sectors	Industries
Industrials	Aerospace & Defense
	Air Freight Logistics
	Airlines
	Building Products
	Commercial Services & Supplies
	Construction & Engineering
	Electrical Equipment
	Industrial Conglomerates
	Machinery
	Marine
	Professional Services
	Road & Rail
	Trading Companies & Distributors
	Transportation Infrastructure
Information Technology	Communications Equipment
	IT Services
	Internet Software & Services
	Semiconductors & Semiconductor Equipment
	Software
	Technology Hardware, Storage & Peripherals
Materials	Chemicals
	Construction Materials
	Containers & Packaging
	Metals & Mining
	Paper & Forest Products
Telecommunication Services	Diversified Telecommunication Services
	Wireless Telecommunication Services

Sectors	Industries
Utilities	Electric Utilities
	Gas Utilities
	Independent Power and Renewable Electricity Producers
	Multi-Utilities
	Water Utilities

Think about the SEGMENTS in your industry. A segment is the "market" that your products or services could be sold into. It is a portioning of an industry into individual markets, each of which encompasses even more specific business activities and needs. Getting to the segment level and knowing what all the relevant segments are cannot be underestimated. We want to be sure that our target audience development is based on reality, and not just a hunch. We could be aiming at too large a target or missing more specific segments that are a better fit for our offering. Getting this nailed down is crucial to the building of a relevant value proposition. Relevance is about specificity – which, by definition, does not mean everyone. So, segment like you mean it!

The sector / industry / segment example below gives a good idea of the organizational structure of beginning to identify your audience. For a complete listing, look at *The North American Industry Classification System (NAICS)* online system for a complete representation of options: www.naics.com.

Once you make your selection of a sector and an industry, you want to be able to narrow it further down by specific segment, region and country. What you're really doing here is "taking aim" at your target. The more specific you can make these targets, the better you will be able to craft a value proposition that speaks directly to the specific segment about the things that matter most to them. The example below is a selection grid that represents a single segment and industry in this manner.

In looking at the "Segment" section, you'll see that there are some pretty specific differences between some of the segments listed. The Consumer segment is going to have a very different set of goals, issues and needs than Network Equipment Providers. You want to ultimately select those segments that make the most sense for the product or service offering that you are bringing to market.

Sector	Industry	Segment	Region	Countries
Industrial	Electronics	Consumer	North America	US, CA (focus on US)
Industrial	Electronics	Medical Devices/Equip	North America	US, CA (focus on US)
Industrial	Electronics	Semi-Conductor & Manufacturing	North America	US, CA (focus on US)
Industrial	Electronics	Industrial Equipment	North America	US, CA (focus on US)
Industrial	Electronics	Office Products and Computers	North America	US, CA (focus on US)
Industrial	Electronics	Network Equip Providers	North America	US, CA (focus on US)

Download Market Segment Template   http://www.valueproposition.expert/marketsegmentation

From Market Segment to the Individual Prospect

The next step is to focus in even closer by deciding which are the key titles and roles that are optimal targets for your offerings. What are the types of individuals at your target companies to whom you want to directly aim your marketing and sales approaches? It is important to pick the titles that are responsible in whole or in part for the decision-making process for purchasing the type of products or services your organization brings to that sector and industry. Think about this a bit to determine who the targets should be. Consider these points:

- Who signs the check?

- Who is responsible for making sure that the right purchase decision is made?

- Who is accountable for getting the outcomes that your product or service provides?

- Who is impacted by your product or service?

- Who else are important stakeholders in deciding on something like this?

- Who influences the decisions, even if they don't have the ultimate authority?

There are literally thousands of titles – and variations of titles. Focus on those titles that have issues, challenges, or goals that your offering can help address. Are there any core or specialty titles that are important to the decision-making process for your product or service? When you look at those titles, how much responsibility do you think that role holds? This will help you identify the decision maker(s), the influencers, and the users of your offer. Your sales team can help you here as well. Who do they call on? Who are the ultimate deciders? Who must not be left out of the sales conversation and purchase process?

It is important to identify their decision roles and their focus. Listing these will help you make the best selection of the key titles to target and will give you the right positioning when you craft your value proposition. First, let's consider the areas of focus:

- Business

- Financial

- Technical

The technical and financial focuses are self-explanatory. Does the role focus on the technical aspects of solving the problem or addressing the buyer's challenge? Who has to handle the financial side of making the purchase? The business focus is a bit different. It is more about either the operational and / or strategic side of things, looking at the business as a whole. It could also be even more focused on a single business unit within the larger organization. While there are titles that may be looking at your offering from all three focus areas, you should select what you believe is their primary focus.

So, when you start to consider titles, here are the key areas to be sure you cover:

Decision Roles Areas include:

- Business Decision Maker

- Business Influencer

- Technical Decision Maker

- Technical Recommender / Influencer

- Financial Decision Maker

- Financial Influencer

The Influencer typically provides research, information, and opinions that contribute in a material way to the purchasing process. In mid-size and larger organizations, they are responsible for a large part of the information gathering needed to evaluate the product or service.

A completed example is presented below. You may have many titles overall – but you want to select and group the *key titles* at whom you will be aiming your value proposition. You may be thinking "Hey, some of these titles are probably coming at this decision from very different points-of-view." Yes – and that means you may have to tweak your ultimate value proposition for them or position it differently. The good news is that the **Value Proposition Platform** you are building here can easily be adjusted as needed for the differences.

One more important consideration you need to make is when you include the Chief Executive Officer and/or the Chief Operating Officer, or the Chief Financial Officer – or any of the other "Chiefs" out there. In the case of the CEO or COO, think of them as being primarily focused on the larger business from both a strategic and operational point-of-view. They are guiding the overall direction across the company and may or may not be directly involved in your product or service purchase decision. So, don't just arbitrarily add them – as messaging to them should have a much different focus than to lower titles in the company. Is the purchase decision about something that is significant to the overall direction of the organization? Is it part of the funding provided for a major strategic initiative? What is the size of the organizations that you are targeting? In small and medium sized businesses, they may be involved in many more of these decisions directly than in an enterprise company.

As far as the CFO, you can count on the fact that if your offering has a high-ticket value, he or she will definitely weigh in. But if not, you will need to plan for a senior financial person or budget holder to be a key influencer. The one that holds the purse strings can be a deal breaker – never underestimate that! You will need some financial positioning added to your core value proposition to take care of this. The table below outlines some typical targets to consider for your audience – including their decision role and focus.

Titles/Roles to Target

Title	Degree of Responsibility	Department	Decision Role	Focus
COO	Operational Head	Operations	Technical Decision Maker	Technical
CIO, CTO	Operational Head	IS/IT	Technical Decision Maker	Technical
CISO (Info/Security Officer)	Operational Head	Security	Technical Decision Maker	Technical
VP of IT	Division Head	IS/IT	Technical Decision Maker	Technical
Director of IT	Department Head	IS/IT	Technical Influencer	Technical
VP Security	Division Head	Security	Technical / Business Decision Maker	Technical
Dir of Information Systems	Department Head	IS/IT	Technical Influencer	Technical
CMO	Organizational Head	Marketing	Decision Maker	Business
VP Marketing	Division Head	Marketing	Decision Maker	Business
VP Sales	Division Head	Sales	Decision Maker	Business
Chief Sales Officer	Organizational Head	Sales	Decision Maker	Business
Dir of Marketing, etc.	Department Head	Marketing	Business Influencer	Business
Marketing Manager, etc.	Individual Contributor /Team Lead	Marketing	Business Influencer	Business

Title	Degree of Responsibility	Department	Decision Role	Focus
Sales Manager, etc.	Individual Contributor /Team Lead	Sales	Business Influencer	Business
CFO	Finance	Finance	Business Decision Maker	Business
VP Finance	Division Head	Finance	Business Decision Maker	Business
Dir of Finance	Department Head	Finance	Business Influencer	Business
Chief Supply Chain Officer	Organizational Head	Supply Chain	Business Decision Maker	Business
VP Supply Chain	Division Head	Supply Chain	Business Decision Maker	Business
Chief Procurement Officer	Organizational Head	Procurement	Business Decision Maker	Business
VP Procurement	Division Head	Procurement	Business Decision Maker	Business
Dir Procurement	Department Head	Procurement	Business Influencer	Business
Manager of Procurement	Individual Contributor /Team Lead	Procurement	Business Influencer	Business

Download Target Title Template   http://www.valueproposition.expert/targettitles

Fill out the template, and then figure out which of the titles represented there are the most important decision makers and influencers for your selected segments. Notice if some of them may be important for some segments, but not others. Set aside those segments that are not part of your core target audience. Later, you can make adjustments to account for their different orientation or environment.

Business Issues

Now you know WHERE and WHOM you are aiming. The next component is to identify the key business issues these buyers have that you want to address with your offering. Business issues include the following:

- Problems they want to solve

- Changes they want to make

- Challenges they have in their own markets

- Needs they have not been able to successfully address

- Goals they want to reach

You want to identify and list these business issues, because you will be using them in the **Buyer Objective Statement** portion of your value proposition. Think about them from the frame of reference of the titles that you selected and their areas of responsibility and focus. Here are some more specific examples:

- **Reduce customer churn**—Sales, Marketing, Business Development, and senior executives all care about this issue

- **Improve productivity**—Chief Operating Officer has this in mind

- **Break down the silos between our divisions**—CEO/COOs worry about silos

- **Increase data security of our customers' information**—This is a worry of the technical people in the IT group.

- **Increase lead conversion from our website**—Marketing owns this worry

Generate a list for your selected decision makers. Then look at your influencer titles and think about whether there are additional issues specific to them that come into play, or is there another aspect of the business issues that the influencers might also be thinking about? Remember, the trend for medium to larger businesses is to have multiple people being part of the buying team. You want to be sure to consider how that impacts the business issues you want to link your value proposition to.

Download Business Issues Template   http://www.valueproposition.expert/businessissues

Let's return to our real examples now, to see what they uncovered for business issues for their target audience.

MediaConvo, Inc.		Version: Marketing	Value Proposition Platform	
SECTOR: Technology	**PRIMARY INDUSTRY**	Information Technology	**SEGMENTS:**	Technology Hardware, Software, and Peripherals
TARGET	**DECISION MAKER TITLES:**	Chief Marketing Officer, VP Marketing, VP Product Marketing, Director of Analyst Relations	**INFLUENCER TITLES:**	Marketing Manager, Public Relations Manager, Analyst Relations Manager, Public Relations Agency, Product Manager
BUSINESS ISSUES	1	Need to know what customers are thinking and what trends are in a timely manner.		
	2	Content about our brand is being created by people external to our company and we don't always know what they are saying.		
	3	Traditional media research tools are not effective for consumer-generated media.		
	4	Must prove to senior executives that we are being successful.		
	5	Protect corporate reputation by understanding impact of our brand in all our markets.		
	6	Don't have a standardized and automated way to collect mentions—very labor intensive pulling from multiple systems and individual research		

The initial brainstorm list of potential business issues is listed above. After discussion and refinement, the final set of issues were:

- Require timely insight on consumer opinions and trends

- Wonder about the impact of consumer-generated media on their brands

- Realize traditional research tools are losing effectiveness

- Must demonstrate measurable success to senior executives

Pay special attention to the business issues here. These issues come from interviews with the customers, from roundtables with the sales team, from competitive analysis, and from the list of customer language included in Chapter 4. Refining them down to this consolidated list will help in the actual drafting of the value proposition, as well as some of the supporting talking points that you will be building into the final **Value Proposition Platform**.

Top Line Sales Example

For this company, a brainstorm list of business issues was created with a Sales Vice President (the main target title). The initial list was too long for the core value proposition. Here were the results of their brainstorm on buyer issues:

- Insufficient sales results

- Mixed results landing larger deals

- Lacking time to focus on strategic account development

- Few people resources

- Resources lack skills to go after large customers

- Customer retention of large accounts

- Fragmented plans for account expansion

- Limited sales tools, processes, methodologies and know-how to differentiate from the competition

- Problems with sales people pursuing large accounts to closure. (Focus, organization, leadership, know-how.)

- Problems with sales people not understanding how to expand large current customers.

This list was pared down to the top five business issues for Top Line Sales' audience analysis:

Top Line Sales		Version: VP of Sales	Value Proposition Platform	
SECTOR: Technology	**PRIMARY INDUSTRY**	Information Technology companies and other B2B companies	**SEGMENTS:**	Technology, software (SaaS), storage & peripherals, manufacturing, printing, healthcare, services
TARGET	**DECISION MAKER TITLES:**	VP Sales, VP of Sales and Marketing, Director of Sales CEO, Business Owner	**INFLUENCER TITLES:**	N/A
BUSINESS ISSUES	1 Our sales results are not good enough. 2 I don't have time to focus on strategic account development. 3 My team lacks skills to pursue, close, expand and retain large accounts. 4 We don't do a good job of differentiating from the competition. 5 My team is inconsistent in landing larger deals.			

Download Value Proposition Platform™ Template	**http://www.valueproposition.expert/valpropplatform**

Buyer Personas: Another Kind of Audience Segmenting

Another approach that can help really define your target audience is the creation of **Buyer Personas.** A persona can help you get a better handle on the motivations of the buyer in a different way.

Definition: Buyer Persona

Built from the real words of real buyers, a buyer persona tells you what prospective customers are thinking and doing as they weigh their options to address a problem that your company resolves. Much more than a one-dimensional profile of the people you need to influence or a map of their journey, actionable buyer personas reveal insights about your buyers' decisions — the specific attitudes, concerns and criteria that drive prospective customers to choose you, your competitor, or the status quo.

Source: The Buyer Persona Institute (www.buyerpersona.com)

Perhaps you have conducted buyer persona research and wonder how to include personas in your value proposition development. Or maybe you do not have personas and wonder if you should, and if so—should you do that research as part of your value proposition project?

To get a highly credible position on that question, I interviewed Julie Schwartz, Senior Vice President, Research and Thought Leadership at ITSMA, the Information Technology Services Marketing Association (www.itsma.com). We started with her take on buyer personas:

"We think of a buyer persona as being an example of a customer who represents a group of buyers. You use the buyer persona, not to tag people and say they're this persona, or they're that persona. You use it to understand more about what motivates buyers to choose your solution. Also, how to persuade them to choose you, rather than a competitor or staying with the status quo. The important thing for people to understand, and the way that I hear it misused so much is, it's not a person or even a group of people. It's a marketing concept."

You don't label actual buyers with a persona as you would do with a job title, for example. A job title is more like a buyer profile, a generic description of that type of buyer, where the CIO at one company looks like the CIO from any other company. A buyer profile can be developed from readily available survey research data, the kind that everybody has. In contrast, Julie says, a buyer persona is all about "what the buyer is trying to *accomplish*. They provide deep insights into when, how and why people are going to buy a particular solution."

The Buyer Persona Institute approaches this from a very buyer-centric perspective. Do not create a persona for every title, in every industry, in every segment. Otherwise you'd end up with hundreds of personas, which will get in the way of doing actual marketing and selling! Building out personas also benefits from real focus – just on those core buyer decision makers or titles that make up the main target audience. You can also address other titles with a modified version or add personas as you need them. Getting at the needs and challenges of buyers with personas is informed by what The Persona Institute calls the ***5 Rings of Buying Insight***™. These factors outlined below get at the heart of what motivates your buyer and can be invaluable to developing a buyer-focused **Value Proposition Platform**.

5 RINGS of BUYING INSIGHT™

| PRIORITY INITIATIVES | SUCCESS FACTORS | PERCEIVED BARRIERS | BUYER'S JOURNEY | DECISION CRITERIA |

Source: The Buyer Persona Institute (www.buyerpersona.com)

Here is an example of some highlights of a sample buyer persona to help you visualize how it works.

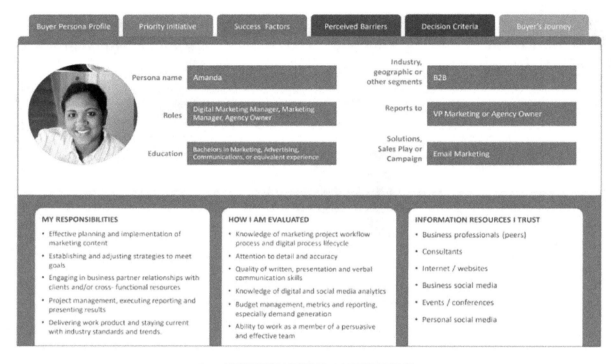

The persona really lays out a comprehensive view of this type of person, what they think, feel, and do – including decision making, initiatives, and a host of highly targeted information.

You will know a great deal about a buyer persona's business issues and objectives that can help you articulate an "outside-in" value perspective and assist you in creating value drivers (the key value points in a buyer's mind throughout their decision-making process), and the proof your target needs to back up your statement. Even more important, you will know a lot about the buyer's journey that this persona tends to follow. This becomes most important as you begin to translate your **Value Proposition Platform** into specific marketing tools, sales materials and a playbook. According to Julie Schwartz, "The focus is more on the buyer decision process, not the buyer. The reason why you use buyer personas is to guide value propositions, crafting messages, and putting together campaigns." Best of all, you can really extend the use of personas across a range of marketing and sales assets.

Sending the Personas to Work

Personas Drive Core Messages	Buyer-Focused Value Propositions	Messaging Platform
Focus on core personas: • Key decision makers • Top influencers	Build main value prop: • Variations by persona • Value drivers • Quantification • Proof	Create a messaging playbook: • Value props • Elevator pitch • Targeted discovery • Objections • Proof • Content assets

Julie did some research recently about pitfalls in creating and using buyer personas. She found three core issues that most marketers have when it comes to buyer persona work:

- "They didn't create buyer personas, they created a profile."

- "They didn't change their marketing strategy and processes to incorporate the buyer personas."

- "They had no plan for 'How do we turn these insights from the buyer personas into actions?' "

If you're worried about the cost or time commitment to conduct buyer persona research, Julie offers encouragement:

> *"My opinion is there's no excuse not to do this kind of research,*
> *because the benefits far outweigh the costs. It is differentiating.*
> *It will give you a competitive advantage.*
>
> *The beauty of buyer personas is that it's a technique to keep you focused*
> *on the buyers' issues, using the buyers' language. It's outside-in, rather*
> *than that inside-out marketing which focuses only on the product or*
> *service. It's client-centric. It helps you get rid of the jargon, the marketing-*
> *speak. It's more likely that the messages derived from personas are*
> *going to attract and retain attention and will be much more relevant."*

A final thought about buyer personas. If you want very practical help to conduct your own research, visit the Buyer Persona Institute. As of this writing, you can download free templates to guide your interview process, read about "The Five Rings of Buyer Insight," and sign up for an online Masterclass to learn everything you should know about how to do your buyer persona research.

Download Buyer Persona Infographic	www.buyerpersona.com/buyer-persona-infographic
Download Buyer Persona Templates	www.buyerpersona.com/buyer-persona-template

Now you have all the components necessary to begin drafting the actual value proposition statement. Let's run through the list:

- Sector defined

- Industry defined

- Core segments defined

- Decision Maker Titles defined (Business, Technical, and Financial)

- Influencer Titles defined (Business, Technical, and Financial)

- Buyer Insight Research (what are their needs, issues, challenges, goals?)

- Buyer Personas (an option for narrowing in on specific types of people)

Review all the pieces above so that your draft speaks directly to these elements and incorporates them into the intent and language of your statement. It's all about the buyer, and soon you will be working on statements that will reflect their world, in their language.

VALUE POINTS

The buyers in our research said only two-thirds of value propositions were at all relevant. The highest were only 71% relevant, and the lowest were only 30% relevant. The scope of opportunity for improvement in the buying process by improving the value proposition is enormous!

To start improving your value prop, you need a deep understanding of your target audience. Consider Buyer Persona research to really get at what motivates and drivers your buyers' decision-making process.

If you serve multiple industries, or if you have multiple products and services, you may need a variety of value propositions. A foundational Value Proposition Platform gives you a base to pivot to different segments as needed. No blank page to start with!

Understanding the Buyer's Objective

FROM THE RESEARCH: AVOID COMMON WEAKNESSES!

Our buyers were very specific about the weaknesses they observed among the value propositions that they had seen during their various buying journeys in their real-life experiences. We asked our survey respondents to select the predominant weaknesses they experienced in the value propositions they considered: (after each weakness is the percentage of respondents).

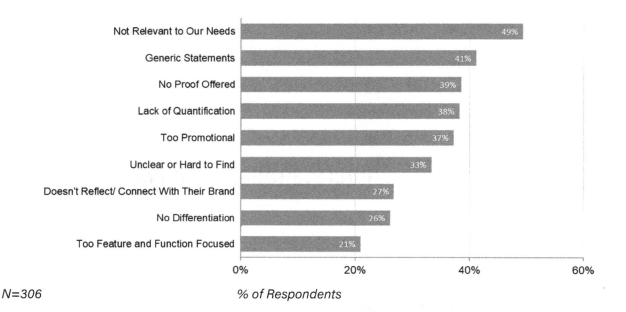

N=306   % of Respondents

Some of these weaknesses are especially important to avoid as you are working on your statement of the buyer's objective. That statement must be completely relevant to the buyers' needs and interests. It can't be generic. In fact, it must be stated in words that the buyers themselves use in talking about what they want and need from a company like yours. And it must be clear and easy to find in your marketing and sales materials, including sales proposals and conversations with sales people.

Now it's time to craft your statement of the buyer's objective when they turn to your company. The focus here is to write a statement that reflects the buyer's point of view and enhance relevance. The goal is to make sure that they don't turn to one of your competitors. So, what are they looking for?

One of the challenges in looking at value propositions is to actually find a set of buyer objectives. Let's look at some specific examples. These have been collected from some live websites over the past few years. The business names and product/service names have been masked, so we can focus on the value propositions themselves.

Example 1

Unique Value Proposition

We are a company dedicated to uniform and logistics in the civilian agency, emergency service, and military markets. What we provide our customer that makes us different from our competitors is:

Big Enough To Deliver, Small Enough To Care

While remaining a family business, we have the organizational and the financial resources to execute some of the largest uniform and personal equipment management projects in the world and the flexibility to tailor them to our customers' expectations. Our solutions are not "cookie cutter" ones. Whether the customer is a fire department in Spain or a public agency in the U.K. or a military customer in the United States, we analyze customer needs, then design a product of [PRODUCT NAME] shown on the following pages.

Commitment To Long-Term Partnerships

This means a focus in our customer relationships on more than "the sale." We wish to foster a close working relationship to build trust. With trust, comes long-term partnerships that last long after the typical product sale. For example, joint working committees between [COMPANY] and its customers are an essential part of our business processes. Openness in sharing ideas to improve joint business processes can only occur when trust is developed. [SERVICE NAME] is our most ambitious expression of this commitment.

Dedicated Internal Research And Development

[COMPANY NAME] is the only company in the world in our industry with dedicated staff working on fundamental research, not gimmicks or do-dads. One of the few with as many as 35 patents, ranging from materials to pattern design. In the end, our customers have a simple feeling about [COMPANY NAME]—trust. They have confidence in our results because we work together as an internal team and as a partner with them to deliver the right solution for them.

Observations

Generic statements: "Big enough to deliver, small enough to care," "family business," not "cookie cutter, "partnership," "trust"

No proof offered: for any of the generic claims

Lack of Quantification: except for the number of patents (which is irrelevant to the buyer unless its relevance is explained)

Too promotional: it's all about the company, not about their buyers. They've used "We" or "our" twelve times in this short statement!

So where did this company go wrong? They are probably close to the truth about their buyers. They've mentioned "confidence in our results" because they work as a partner with our buyers. They mention "joint working committees." So, they probably do many things that are designed to build trust with their customers. But they certainly don't capture it with headlines like the ones they've chosen. The real question that is not answered here is, what is the trust really about? What do the buyers need or want that they will trust the company to deliver?

First, they're trying to appeal to all of their buyers with one statement. They have three buyer market segments: civilian agencies, emergency services, and military. They sell both uniforms and logistics services -- very different things. They also manage both uniforms and "personal equipment;" unclear whether that means sale of personal equipment or just delivery to the right places at the right times. They could probably benefit from a value proposition dedicated to *each* market segment, and perhaps some differentiation between products they sell and services they deliver.

Here's what we have learned about them specifically, just from the statement they've written:

- They serve customers of all sizes all over the world—even giant customers like the US military. No matter how big or small the customer, the company has the capacity to analyze their needs and provide them with a custom solution.

- They provide a solution called [PRODUCT NAME], which is their "most ambitious expression" of close working relationships to build trust. It is characterized by joint working committees between the company and the customer after the sale.

- The company is the only company in the world in its industry (idea: add a citation of a third party stating this about them if they have it).

- Unlike its competitors, the company employs a dedicated research and development team (Idea: indicate % of revenue devoted to R&D) working on the fundamentals of materials and pattern design, for which we hold 35 patents (idea: give a couple of meaningful examples).

Identifying Targeted Language

There's another way to help them get at how their buyers might express their needs. One of the most important things to understand about your target audience is the language they typically use when talking about their needs. Identify and utilize key words that your prospects and customers use to describe their situations, goals, needs and business pain, and you will increase relevance. The words are crucial, as they speak to your credibility, and demonstrate your knowledge of their situation. You want to embed them in your **Buyer Objective Statement**. This table relates to our previous example company, the uniform and logistics provider.

Issue Words	Pain Words	Goal Words	Challenge Words
Low Profit Margin	Waste	Confidence to Meet Deadlines	Complexity
Turn-Around Time	Shrink	Long-Term Solution	Wearability
Fear of Failure to Meet Deadlines	Employee Discomfort Complaints	Cost Retention	Churn

Even based on these few examples, here's how they might craft a buyer's objective:

"In today's military environment, equipping personnel with uniforms and personal equipment is extremely complex. Advances in wearable technology and the weight, durability, and general behavior of materials and fabrics make the standard knowledge of what's available very outdated. Uniform specifiers need to know not only all the most current options, but also what's on the horizon to ensure that the purchase's usable lifetime is not short-term. Given the variability in the environments personnel must

> *be ready for, options for custom solutions for comfort as well as overall uniformity are crucial. Also important is the ability to deliver uniforms and equipment globally, wherever and whenever they are needed."*

Think through and pull the targeted language you've identified and included in your business needs research for your target audience. The most important thing to keep in mind when drafting the Buyer Objective Statement is the "perspective" needed for the statement. It should not be your company's perspective.

The biggest challenge in creating value propositions is making enough room in your head to immerse yourself in what the buyer experience is: how they want to be helped, and what language they would use to describe it. We typically only think about this from our own company point of view – our product can do this, this and this, and you NEED it! Breaking it into pieces and getting clear on what the perspective needs to be for each piece, gives you the space to hone in on a finely targeted message that will make sense to the buyer. It makes it easier for them to relate to your value proposition. At its most successful, the buyer will "recognize" themselves when they read or hear it.

Here's an excerpt from another value proposition that does include a Buyer Objective Statement – note the bold text for this statement.

Example 2

Value Proposition

> *Today, enterprises need a paradigm shift to continue delivering value for a promising tomorrow. Transformative trends are changing the business landscape time and again.* **It is a daunting task to justify roles and track business outcomes from technology investments. Enterprises**

are finding it difficult to meet challenges such as rising stakeholder expectations, compliance frameworks, market volatility, need for innovation, social commerce, pervasive computing, mobile workforce, and environmental concerns. *Enterprise-wide insight, efficient analytics, unified databases, integrated processes, and streamlined workflows to ensure real-time collaboration and intelligent decision-making are imperative.*

At the [COMPANY DIVISION NAME] we combine the power of [COMPANY]'s best-of-breed products with our deep expertise and wide experience to deliver measurable business value to our clients. Our clients leverage our expertise in consulting, technology and sourcing to transform their business and create outcomes in three key areas: business transformation, accelerated innovation and efficient operations.

The highlighted text constitutes the buyer's objective. The strength in this part of the value proposition is that the selling company clearly expresses a set of needs from the buyer's point of view, the buyer being "enterprises." They are having trouble justifying roles and tracking business outcomes from their investments in technology. They are also finding it difficult to meet a laundry list of problems that the seller proposes to solve for them. The next sentence is part buyer objective and part seller's offer—probably more on the seller's offer side, because it states in the seller's language what the buyers need. That's what the sellers think they need, but we don't know, really, if that's what the buyers want.

Let's take another look at the buyer's objective. Its weakness is that it's not stated in the kind of language that real buyers might use. They wouldn't come up with that kind of a sentence, lumping all these things together. Very different buyers make those statements. The CEO and CFO talk about stakeholder expectations. IT probably manages the compliance frameworks. Market volatility concerns senior management as well as Marketing, Product Development, Business Development, and Human Resources. I could go on, but the point is "enterprises" are not buyers. Who buys enterprise software? The same buyers who responded to my survey! Executives of business units, IT, and finance, as well as consultants and other advisors. They are sophisticated buyers with a highly-developed sense of what is relevant to their specific business needs in a value proposition.

As you work on your own value proposition, make it a priority to find the buyer's language. Remember this rule: simplicity is your friend. And its corollary: complexity is your enemy. If your audience needs to "figure out" your value proposition, they won't – and you've lost them.

How to get started

Take your buyer needs that you created when developing your target audience research and translate that into a statement that is entirely about the buyer.

Instructions for the Buyer Objective Statement

1   Draft a 1 – 3 sentence statement that states the buyer's need, challenge, situation or problem.

2   Use language that they would use to describe themselves (embed the keywords you have identified through your buyer research).

3   Word the objective in a way that you can later apply your own offer to it in specific terms (business needs).

You will go through multiple drafts of this. That's exactly how to do it! You want to be really comfortable with the buyer statement BEFORE you start the next section which is your company's offer.

Do not move ahead, even if you think you can do this all at once. You can't. If you skip over this first section, or do it quickly and without much thought, your value proposition is going to end up being weak and more focused on your company than on your buyer. Hey, you already know how to write a value prop that is all about your offer! Your goal now is to cross over and talk about it from the buyer side. Why? Relevancy and differentiation. Don't forget the prize!

Here are some examples of Buyer Objective Statements so you can get an idea of direction. Notice that they do NOT include anything about the product or service. It is crucial that you don't let your company offering creep into the Buyer Objective Statement. That comes next. When you are done, you'll have a grouping of three sets of statements: Buyer Objective, Company Offer, and Differentiator. Ultimately, you will boil them down into a single tight statement, but for now let's keep focused section by section. As you read the following samples, notice the issues that are presented. See if you can get an idea of WHO the buyers are as described in this statement. Buyers should be able to see themselves (the mirror) in this statement – and calling out who the buyers are in the actual statement makes this easier and more direct.

Sample 1:

> *Employers, insurers and claims paying organizations are rightly concerned with the increased costs of their workers' compensation, group health, and auto liability programs – but their cost control efforts may not generate the desired goal. Payer issues include increased claims volumes, medical cost containment, and medical abuse and overuse. Meanwhile employers are dealing with rapidly escalating total costs and rising claims severity.*

Sample 2:

IT organizations across every industry who are trying to lower the cost and risk of managing their critical applications should ask themselves the following questions:

- *What is the cost of having your application down for an extra hour as you try to deploy a new version?*

- *How much time have you spent trying to troubleshoot a problem where you were working in the dark for a lack of data?*

- *Does your current solution scale across all your systems and meet your growth goals?*

As you can see in both samples, the buyer is called out, and the issues are clear, simple and direct. You do not need a translator to figure out what the business needs are – and you might not even be a member of either industry.

Now let's go back to our case study examples, MediaConvo, Inc., and Top Line Sales.

Example: MediaConvo, Inc.

Target: Marketing Departments

Tuning into the voice of your market is becoming more difficult due to the millions of consumer-to-consumer conversations that are diluting the impact of your company's marketing programs. In today's Influence 2.0 world, consumers are creating their own brand dialogue by blending your product messaging with their own experiences and opinions, other consumers' input, and traditional media content. Can you afford to be out of sync with your market?

Notice how the statement directly addresses the audience with the word "you" as well as the discipline the buyer is engaged in: product messaging, brand dialogue. It's easy to figure out that this is aimed at Marketing because it is talking about areas that Marketing is responsible for. A vice president of marketing will easily be able to recognize themselves in "the mirror" of that buyer audience!

Example: Top Line Sales

Target: Vice President, Sales

When was the last time each of your team members closed a seven-figure contract? Despite the best sales talent, many high potential, critical deals get whittled down or are lost completely. Large opportunities are complex and require a carefully orchestrated approach to identify, develop and win.

This Buyer Objective Statement challenges the target audience right from the beginning. The answer to that question touches on a key pain point faced by many small and medium business executives.

Extended Example: MediaConvo, Inc. Public Relations Version

MediaConvo, Inc. had two major target audience segments: Marketing departments and Public Relations departments. So, the CMO decided that they really needed two versions of their value proposition because each segment had different issues and used different language.

Presented below is a set of four drafts that got us to the final Public Relations version of the buyer statement. The last version became the Buyer's Objective Statement for the value proposition directed to MediaConvo's target of Public Relations buyers.

Draft 1 PR Buyer Objective

We started with two alternatives. Each statement has 3 sentences. I've separated them and marked in boldface the sentences that are different in each version.

> **The voice of the media has become fragmented across a complex array of sources including blogs, message boards, Usenet news groups, online opinion/review sites in addition to traditional media outlets.**

> **In today's media remix culture, consumers are creating their own brand dialogue by blending your product messaging with their own experiences and opinions, other consumers' input, and mainstream media content.**

> *PR professionals need to reduce the complexity and hone in on just the relevant voices to accurately track and measure key message pick up and corporate reputation.*

Alternate #2

> **If a single voice shares an opinion on the internet and your company is not there to hear it, does it make a sound?**

In today's media remix culture, journalists are tuning into those voices, sourcing stories from bloggers while bloggers comment on stories in mainstream media, creating an "echo chamber" effect that amplifies the impact of news, good and bad.

PR professionals need to reduce the complexity and hone in on just the relevant voices to accurately track and measure key message pick up and corporate reputation.

Draft 2 PR Buyer Objective

*The voice of the media has become fragmented **with journalists sourcing stories from bloggers while bloggers comment on stories in mainstream media, amplifying the impact of good and bad news.***

*In today's media remix culture, consumers are creating their own brand dialogue by **blending product messaging** with their own experiences and opinions, other consumers' input, and mainstream media content.*

*PR professionals need to reduce the complexity and **focus on** just the relevant voices to accurately track and measure key message pick up and corporate reputation.*

In this revision, we've decided against the play on words introduction "if a tree falls in the forest and no one hears it, does it make a sound?" It was a great way to get our heads in the topic, but we needed to be sure not to take on the baggage that comes with a slogan like that. We like "the voice of the media has become fragmented," and "today's media remix culture," as well as address the PR professional's needs.

Draft 3: PR Value Proposition

> *The voice of the media has become fragmented **across a complex array of sources including blogs, message boards, Usenet newsgroups, online opinion/review sites and traditional outlets.***

> *In today's media remix culture, consumers are creating their own brand dialogue by blending your product messaging with their own experiences and opinions, other consumers' input, and mainstream media content.*

> **Can you afford to be out of sync with your market?**

In the next revision, we're getting much more specific about how the voice of the media has become fragmented and what consumers are doing in the media remix culture. We are also tightening the language along the way. The key addition in this version is a totally new concept about the PR professional's fear—being "out of sync" with their market! It puts a finger squarely in the middle of the "anxiety" that PR professionals were feeling at the time we were working on this project. Social media was still fairly new, and there was no easy way to figure out who and what was being said without enormous manual searching and gathering.

Final Public Relations Buyer Objective Statement

> *The voice of the media has become fragmented across a complex array of sources with the addition of blogs, message boards, Usenet newsgroups, and online opinion/review sites.*

> *In today's **Influence 2.0 world, these sources become entwined as journalists pick up story ideas from bloggers and bloggers remark on mainstream media and corporate content.***

> *This new brand dialogue demands an understanding of the consumer experience above and beyond traditional tracking of key message pickup.*

> *Can you afford to be out of sync with your market?*

In this final revision, we tightened up the first point. We made the second point much more concrete by replacing "consumers" with "journalists and bloggers" and defining their sources as "mainstream media and corporate content." This statement is simpler and much more alive than the former generic language. Then we added a new sentence to make a bridge from what the journalists and bloggers are doing to what the PR professionals need to avoid - being out of sync with their market, the core worry of public relations professionals at the time.

Hopefully, this example of a revision process helps you see how revisions will get you closer and closer to the most relevant language for each audience. You are striving for specific language aimed at specific audience targets. This process helps you avoid generic statements and words.

Once you're satisfied with your statement of the buyer's objective, you're ready to move on to rebuilding your **Company Offer Statement** for your new value proposition. You are probably going to have to tighten it up or make some changes because you want to include only that which plugs directly into this new **Buyer Objective Statement**.

VALUE POINTS

The top weaknesses associated with the Buyer Objective Statement include: Not relevant to the buyers' needs; generic statements; and unclear or hard to find buyer concerns.

Identifying key words that buyers use to describe their situations, goals, needs, and business pain is an important first step in crafting a Buyer Objective Statement.

You will need different Buyer Objective Statements for different buying groups or audiences or for major differences among products and services.

Beware of industry jargon and your own internal company-speak, instead make sure to research and use buyer language to ensure relevance.

7

Retooling Your Offer

FROM THE RESEARCH: PERSONALIZE TO THE BUYER

Our respondents placed higher weight on value propositions that address Organizational Benefits versus Personal Benefits (59% vs. 41%), and they expected that importance to grow to 62% vs. 39% in the next two years. However, 62% of respondents said that lack of clear value to them can reduce the likelihood that they would support a vendor's offer. All respondents said that lack of clear value to them can reduce the likelihood of their support for a vendor's offer by 58%.

Vendor personalization is most desired in three areas:

- By Product/Service Features (19%)

- My Primary Decision Interest (technical, financial and/or business impact) (17%)

- Areas of Risk, Control and Rewards (practicality, recognition, hassle free implementation, benefits desired) (17%)

Based on this buyer information, it seems quite important to address both organizational benefits as well as personal benefits to the buyers. You are well on your way beginning with the **Buyer Objective Statement**. The key is to extend that as you create your **Company Offer Statement**.

You want the Offer Statement to communicate HOW your offer is going to address the specific business needs of your buyer. You want this statement to precisely state the primary reasons that your offer can help them. Be careful here. You don't want to include everything there is to tell about your offering. Why? Because your buyers don't *care* about everything! They only care about what is relevant to their own needs. Furthermore, it must be compelling because you are trying to set yourself apart and gain their attention. You want them to say "Yes, that's me!" when they hear this statement. Often, this section will get morphed into the core part of an elevator speech. Think about the one or two things about your solution to their business needs that you want them to have top-of-mind. This isn't about product features. This is about the *value* of the solution you are offering to them. Beware of stuffing features in here to prove value. The value is in your ability to MEET THEIR NEEDS. Features are merely a means to that end. What value will they derive from adopting your solution?

Another essential aspect of this section is making sure your Offer Statement is understandable to your target market. Understandability cannot be overlooked here. Just because your marketing and sales people understand it, there is no guarantee that your new prospects or existing customers do. Acronyms, or very technical language, or internal company jargon typically end up in this section. It complicates the statement unnecessarily. If your audience doesn't know what it means, many of them won't bother to find out – they will just move on.

Also, be sure to weed out all traces of "marketing-speak." By that I mean generic, fluffy marketing language that doesn't mean anything specific. If it doesn't directly apply to the business needs in the Buyer Objective, then it doesn't belong in the Offer Statement. It should be tight, clear, and in the language of the buyer. value propositions do not come with "translators," so don't put a prospect in the position of needing one.

Finally, you need to be able to quantify any of the claims you make in this section. If you say that you increase productivity, then you need to be able to say by how much with a specific number or a range. If you can't state it, it is not credible to the buyer. Anyone can say they increase productivity or reduce costs or help with generating additional revenue. Without **Quantification**, it isn't unique or differentiating – it is vague, "me too" language that ends up just being "marketing-speak." Make it real by being specific and backing it up. Otherwise, it simply isn't believable, and therefore has no place in your offer.

With all those additional suggestions and guidelines, let's work on the Offer Statement. You'll do multiple drafts of this section – and to keep on track, refer to your latest Buyer Objective Statement so that you are sure that you are connecting your offer there. A good rule of thumb in crafting this section is to ask the following: Can everything in our Offer Statement be linked back to the buyer needs we have identified? If not, leave that piece out. Don't stuff your Offer Statement with things that are not relevant to the buyer's needs.

Instructions for the Offer Statement

1   1 – 3 sentence statement that describes your offer.

2   Your offer must specifically address your Buyer Objective – it must tie back to the business needs stated there.

3 Beware of jargon or acronyms that your buyer may not know, or generic terms that don't provide specific enough information.

4 Keep it simple and direct – resist the urge to put in everything you know about your offer. Stick to the main aspects. You will have the opportunity to get down into the details in your marketing and sales materials later.

Here are some real examples of Offer Statements to give you an idea of the direction to go in. Notice that they stay pretty high level and don't include too much detail. They do not include all the features of the offer. The value proposition is meant to attract buyers. By matching your Offer Statement to the Buyer Objective, you are building the means for that attraction. It is just the beginning of conversation – not the entire conversation.

Example 1:

In response to these client and market needs we have focused our healthcare and professional services resources, along with our technology, information system and work process re-engineering expertise to create and deliver the following business benefits and results:

- *Improve cost efficiencies for claims and patient services by 25%*

- *Increase cost savings by 15% for our customers*

- *Increase patient record accuracy to meet government mandates by 10%*

Example 2:

> [Product Name] is an application deployment and management system that dramatically reduces the time and effort required to launch and manage applications on business-critical servers. Proven to scale across thousands of servers across geographic regions, the system delivers the ability to deploy, troubleshoot, repair, upgrade, operating and manage servers from a single system.

Now let's get back to our own two example companies and look at the development of their Offer Statements.

Example 3: Top Line Sales, Vice President, Sales Version

> We overcome the barriers to winning TOP Line Accounts™ whether they're worth 100K or 10M+. Top Line Sales instills the know-how into your sales organization to identify, cultivate and close strategic account opportunities through a field-proven process that includes the right tools, strategic training and live deal coaching. Our TOP Line Account™ War Room service ensures that your most important account opportunities have the highest level of focus, accountability and momentum all the way through closure. This directed approach increases critical contract close ratios and turns your sales team into strategic "Top Line" sellers.

Example 4: MediaConvo, Inc., Marketing Version

> *MediaConvo, Inc., a market influence analytics company, sifts and interprets the millions of voices at the intersection of consumer-generated and traditional media. Our award-winning platform integrates innovative technology with expert analysis to identify the people, issues and trends impacting your business — at the speed of the market.*

Extended Example: Top Line Sales

The primary goal of a value proposition is to be relevant to the business needs and issues of buyers. So, we must ask ourselves at every turn, does our company offer relate directly to any of the business issues that our target audience identified? Let's see how Top Line Sales measures up. First, let's take another look at their statement and then break it down.

> *We overcome the barriers to winning TOP Line Accounts™ whether they're worth 100K or 10M+. Top Line Sales instills the know-how into your sales organization to identify, cultivate and close strategic account opportunities through a field-proven process that includes the right tools, strategic training and live deal coaching. Our TOP Line Account™ War Room service ensures that your most important account opportunities have the highest level of focus, accountability and momentum all the way through closure. This directed approach increases critical contract close ratios, and turns your sales team into strategic "Top Line" sellers.*

Business Need	Offer Statement Attribute
Our sales results are not good enough.	Instills the know-how into your sales organization to identify, cultivate and close strategic account opportunities.
I don't have time to focus on strategic account development.	Our TOP Line Account™ War Room service ensures that your most important account opportunities have the highest level of focus, accountability and momentum.
My team lacks skills to pursue, close, expand and retain large accounts.	A field-proven process that includes the right tools, strategic training and live deal coaching.
We don't do a good job of differentiating from the competition.	Not applicable.
My team is inconsistent in landing larger deals.	This directed approach increases critical contract close ratios, and turns your sales team into strategic "Top Line" sellers.

In a succinct way, Top Line Sales' Offer Statement covers most of the key business issues. The issue of "not having enough time" is answered indirectly by bringing up the War Room service where Top Line Sales is leading the strategic account development process. The business issue of not delivering good differentiation is not addressed in the Offer Statement. Not every business issue has to be included. It is perfectly appropriate to pick and choose. Frankly, differentiation is a big challenge for many organizations – and it typically takes more than one approach to address it. It makes sense to set this aside in the actual Offer Statement. It may not be a core ingredient of the Top Line Sales approach.

Let's look a bit deeper at the final issue "inconsistency in landing larger deals." The Offer Statement doesn't simply say "we make your team more consistent." Instead, the Offer Statement ups the ante by saying we have a "directed approach" that accomplishes that goal. It's a subtle difference but a critical one. It's like the difference between your freight carrier saying, "we deliver on time" or saying, "in the last 3 years, 98% of our deliveries have been on time." Or your dry cleaner saying, "we'll never lose your clothes," or saying, "we installed an advanced automated inventory tracking system last year to ensure that we never lose an item of clothing."

Please note also that the term TOP Line Accounts™ is a trademarked term. There is careful attention to describe it in a range of ways: a 7-figure account, a strategic account, your most important accounts, a $100,000 account or a $10 million account. She wants her buyers to know it's big—whatever BIG means for them. It's big and complex and not easy to close. It takes time and strategy to close one. You can't close $10 million accounts if you don't have $10 million-dollar products and services to sell. Could you sell $10m of your services or products to the same customer over 10 years? For some clients, quite certainly. For others, that's just not their business model. The size is not as important as the significance. And "TOP Line" phrase puts the emphasis on revenue—income—not cost-cutting. The company owns a big differentiator in its offer language. If you have words of such significance in your keyword inventory, or if you invent them in your value proposition process, use them bravely! And be sure to get trademark protection. (For information on the mechanics of trademarks, go to www.uspto.gov/trademark.)

This company offer is also a good example of personalization, as it is clearly designed to be aimed specifically at a vice president of sales. This person will clearly understand and recognize the organizational benefits because people in that position know how closely their job performance aligns with company success. On the other hand, the business issues relate to the vice president's personal job performance, the performance of their team, and their work / life balance and job satisfaction. It should appear very relevant to the buyer.

Extended Example: MediaConvo, Inc.

First, let's look at the Company Offer of several of MediaConvo's competitors. The information we gathered was based on a competitive messaging scan which gathered taglines, value proposition language (where there was a discernable one), and keywords. The main point for this exercise is for MediaConvo to get a handle on what everyone else in their market space is saying, and to avoid using the same language that its competitors use. They want to differentiate themselves, not just be a 'me too' company amongst a group of like offerings. This activity was a basis for all versions of the MediaConvo value proposition. Let's start by looking at an earlier version (before we started working on it) of MediaConvo's Offer Statement.

MediaConvo Offer:

MediaConvo is the leader in **extracting actionable market knowledge – real-time insight into customer /consumer behaviors and emerging market trends** by monitoring, measuring, and managing the full spectrum of Mainstream Media (MSM) and Consumer Generated Media (CGM) content.

Competitor Offers (key value statements are highlighted)

Competitor B is a market intelligence company that **tracks, analyzes and distills consumer opinions and perceptions of the online world** – consisting of more than 27 million blogs, message boards, opinion sites and other public forums – into insights about companies, products, people and issues.

Competitor C is the leader in word-of-mouth research and planning, **helping companies listen to, measure and act upon the online consumer dialogue affecting their markets.** We uncover and connect remarkably objective, sometimes startling consumer insight to effective strategies that let you influence the way people talk about your brands.

Competitor D's product helps businesses and government organizations succeed by providing market intelligence that delivers a **360-degree view of your company, your**

competitors, and your market. We deliver real-time insight you can use to be more strategic, more competitive, and ultimately more profitable.

Competitor E: Product reputation intelligence enables you to understand how **perceptions found in the media and public opinion affect your company's bottom line,** so you can formulate proactive reputation and brand-management strategies.

Competitor F can **"see" the "peaks of passion" in online conversations to understand customer motivations.** We use a combination of proprietary software and world-class analysts to explore what drives customer behavior. Think of it as quantitative research with the richness of qualitative data but more honest and faster than both.

Competitor G **deciphers valuable business intelligence from the noise of people's own online words**, using an unequaled pairing of online dialogue management expertise and proprietary technology.

Competitor H is the only Internet monitoring company that places an organization's brand at the center of its online business. Competitor H solutions **bridge the gap between security and marketing initiatives to secure brand assets and maximize business performance.**

Competitor I delivers knowledge, collaboration and insight **to help companies understand and improve their reputations**, plan and evaluate their communications programs and sharpen their competitive edge.

As we began to create the company offer for MediaConvo, we had a long list of words and phrases to avoid! In particular, "actionable market knowledge" and "real-time insight" was used by at least five competitors. Clearly those weren't differentiating statements for anyone to use, and MediaConvo for sure!

The next set of information shared below is four drafts of the MediaConvo Company Offer, written for the Public Relations (PR) version. This differs from the Marketing version that you saw above.

Each statement has 3 parts. I've separated them and marked in boldface the parts that change in each version. Notice how the company Offer Statement struggles to state exactly what kind of company MediaConvo is. In thinking back to the initial set of internal interviews done at the start of this project, this was a big issue. Staff people were quite sure that the company was changing, but not entirely sure how to define that change.

Draft 1 PR Value Prop

MediaConvo, Inc., a brand perception analytics company, sifts and interprets the millions of voices at the intersection of consumer-generated and mainstream media.

With Opus, our award-winning platform that combines innovative technology with expert analysis,

you can easily isolate just the relevant voices to uncover the brand insights that drive new business opportunities and protect corporate reputation.

Draft 2 PR Value Prop

MediaConvo, Inc., a brand perception analytics company, sifts and interprets the millions of voices at the intersection of consumer-generated and mainstream media.

With Opus, our award-winning platform that combines innovative technology with expert analysis,

We uncover new business opportunities and identify threats to corporate reputation at the speed of the market.

In draft 2, only the last section is changed, and basically it tries to tighten up the language and capture some key benefits that a buyer might want.

Draft 3 PR Value Prop

MediaConvo, **a market influence analytics company,** *sifts and interprets the millions of voices at the intersection of consumer-generated and mainstream media.*

Our award-winning platform, Opus, integrates innovative technology with expert analysis to uncover new business opportunities and identify threats to corporate reputation — at the speed of PR.

Draft 3 makes a major change in the type of company MediaConvo calls itself, without changing what it does. It strengthens the second section by replacing the word "combines" with "integrates" and replaces the phrase "at the speed of the market" used in the Marketing version of the value prop and replaces it with "at the speed of PR".

Draft 4 PR Value Prop

> *MediaConvo, a market influence analytics company, sifts and interprets the millions of voices at the intersection of consumer-generated and mainstream media.*
>
> *Our award-winning platform, Opus, integrates innovative technology with expert analysis to **identify the people, issues and trends impacting your business — at the speed of the market.***

The final revision replaces some corporate-speak in sentence three ("uncover new business opportunities and identify threats to corporate reputation") with more buyer-friendly language ("to identify the people, issues and trends impacting your business"). The final version also reverts to the original final phrase, "at the speed of the market." This change was made because the same concept impacts the Marketing department as well as the Public Relations department – the overall speed at which mainstream media and consumer generated media run. It's not different, so the phrase works for both versions and should be consistent in point.

Let's recap the final version:

> *MediaConvo, a market influence analytics company, sifts and interprets the millions of voices at the intersection of consumer-generated and mainstream media. Our award-winning platform, Opus, integrates innovative technology with expert analysis to identify the people, issues and trends impacting your business — at the speed of the market.*

This Company Offer Statement packs a great deal of information in two sentences. Let's break this down by testing it with some key questions:

Who is MediaConvo? A market influence analytics company.

What does that mean? They analyze how different media influence your market

How do they do it? They "sift and interpret" — that means they go through and make sense of the millions of voices that come together where mainstream media (MSM, i.e., journalists) and consumer-generated media (CGM, i.e., bloggers and consumers like you and me) intersect.

From an offering standpoint, they cover both types of media in their product and in their Offer Statement, which none of the other competitors can cover. Note that they avoided using the acronyms MSM and GSM in the final statement. While they may be industry acronyms, there is no guarantee that everyone who consumes this value proposition will know what they mean. Plain English goes a long way to help with value proposition clarity.

How does it help me? They have a tool, a technology platform called Opus, which they use alongside 'expert analysis" (translation: real people with analytical skills) to find the people, issues, and trends that impact your business. And they do this really fast. As fast as the market changes.

As one final test, let's see how this Offer Statement matches up against the business issues that we identified in Chapter 5. Here's the list of MediaConvo's six customer business issues, followed by excerpts from MediaConvo's Buyer Objective Statement that seem to address those issues:

Business Need	Offer Statement Attribute
Need to know what customers are thinking and what trends are in a timely manner.	Identify the people, issues and trends impacting your business — at the speed of the market.
Content about our brand is being created by people external to our company and we don't always know what they are saying.	Sifts and interprets the millions of voices at the intersection of consumer-generated and mainstream media.
Traditional media research tools are not effective for consumer-generated media.	Integrates innovative technology with expert analysis.
Must prove to senior executives that we are being successful.	Identify the people, issues and trends impacting your business.
Protect corporate reputation by understanding impact of our brand in all our markets.	Identify the people, issues and trends impacting your business.
Don't have a standardized and automated way to collect mentions— very labor intensive pulling from multiple systems and individual research.	Sifts and interprets, innovative technology, at the speed of the market.

It could be argued that this Company Offer addresses as many as five of six business issues that the MediaConvo team identified. If you find yourself getting that close just on your Company Offer, you should first consider whether you may have simply restated one or two business issues in several different ways. If you're certain you have not, then congratulate yourself on a job well done! It's not necessary to answer all the business issues in the company offer. Focus on the core issues, the ones that are the most important to your buyer that your offering directly addresses. You'll also have an opportunity to go deeper on them in your **Differentiator**, and you can add some subsidiary needs in your **Value Drivers** to back up the offer statement, along with providing **Quantification** and **Proof**. But you definitely want to cover the key ones in the actual Value Proposition Offer Statement itself.

In the next chapter, you'll be ready to move on to developing the **Differentiator** section of your value proposition. Get ready, because this is usually the hardest part of all!

VALUE POINTS

Buyers say that organizational benefits are more important than personal benefits to them. However, almost two-thirds said that a lack of clear personal value to them would reduce the likelihood that they would support a vendor's offer.

Be sure not to include "everything you know" about your offering in the Offer Statement. Less is more here. Focus on addressing the core business needs of your buyers – you are aiming for relevancy, not a plethora of features and benefits.

You may be surprised when you do a competitive analysis of all your key competitors' marketing language. A comparison of their messaging will reveal many similarities in keywords, phrases and taglines. Identify areas to avoid, and gaps / opportunities where you can develop more differentiating language. Don't write your company offer without completing a competitive grid. It will save you from sounding "me too."

Double-check the final draft of your company offer against the business issues in your audience summary. Be sure you've covered those business needs that you believe are the highest priority for your buyers.

8

Defining True Differentiators

FROM THE RESEARCH: PROMISE ONGOING VALUE!

Vendor value propositions should address a few different types of value they bring to the buyers and their organization. The options are:

ONGOING VALUE: How they are sustainable and will stay/keep things up and running.

ADDED VALUE: How they can enhance your processes, efficiency, effectiveness, insight and performance.

NEW VALUE: How they can help you change the competitive rules to enhance success.

We asked our survey respondents: As you made your purchase decision how much overall weight (sum to 100) did you give to each level of value?

Ongoing Value:	39
Added Value:	29
New Value:	21

As you work on describing the qualities of your product and/or service that make you different from competitors, the biggest challenge is to describe these qualities as *benefits* to the buyers rather than *features* of the product / service. One way to address that is to see if your statement reveals at least one of the three types of value to the buyer, as identified above.

Probably the hardest section to develop in a strong value proposition statement is the **Differentiator**. The word "differentiator" means the following:

The unique features and / or benefits of a product or service that set it apart from competing products or services.

The key word here is UNIQUE. This means it cannot be something that every other competitor has or claims. It needs to set your offer apart, and really give the buyer a solid reason to pick your offer over the available alternatives. Suffice to say, this isn't always easy. Most often, companies stuff as many things as they can think of into the differentiator with the idea that the more they have listed, the better off they are. Wrong! For any differentiator to be valuable, it must be:

- Believable

- Valuable to the buyer

- Specific

- Provable

Of the three components of a strong value proposition, this section, the differentiator, requires real awareness of what your competition is claiming. Let's review the components of the competitive scan that are most relevant to the Differentiator Statement: Tag Line, Key Words, and Competitor Differentiators.

Perform Competitor Messaging Scan

This analysis is worth doing to get an understanding of what other companies are saying in your market space. Scan the language used: tagline, value proposition, differentiators, key words, product / service messaging, and positioning. As part of your company's development of its product or service, there was likely a full competitive analysis done, to ensure that there is a place for the offer and that it brings something to the table that prospects are going to want to purchase. If possible, access that analysis. At the very least, speak to someone who had a hand in the development. This information will be very helpful here. It can help you with actual differences in the product or service itself. But at a minimum, it is necessary to do a "messaging scan" that really focuses on the marketing and sales language used to communicate with buyers. You are looking to identify two things:

1   The words, phrases, and attributes that your competitors use – so you can completely avoid them, to keep from sounding like "me too."

2   Any gaps which may represent opportunities for you to fill in your own messaging to differentiate your offering.

For the purposes of this value proposition work, focus on the unique features, benefits and differences from the other available alternatives. Just beware on focusing on a feature that is currently unique, as the clock is already ticking until a competitor goes after it, and replicates or one-ups it! Focus on value – definable, ongoing value that can be backed up with proof. This is what buyers are really looking for as they evaluate vendor solutions.

If you've done the competitive language scan from Chapter 4, then you will have a good understanding of what your challenges and opportunities for differentiators will be. Be sure to focus on the QUALITY of the differentiator, not the quantity. One or two true, believable, and provable differentiators are worth more than a bunch of generic, vague, "me too" items.

Here are some steps to get you ready to work on your differentiators:

- **Review your competitive messaging scan**

  - Where are there gaps that your offer can cover?

  - Are there any opportunities to "own" a particular feature or benefit?

  - Can we deliver more than what's available from the competitors, or one-up what they are claiming?

- **Restrict to 1 – 3 differentiators at a maximum**

  - It's rare that any legitimate offer truly has more than this.

  - If you must stretch or be vague to claim it, don't.

  - If you can't offer proof, it's not going to be viewed as important or real.

- **Must be truly differentiating**

    - It must be provable – objective third-party proof is best.

    - It should not be already done by primary competitors.

    - Focus on overall value, not the details of the features or benefits.

    - Include at least one of the three types of value (ongoing, added, or new).

Instructions for Developing Differentiators

1   Develop 1-3 differentiating points that are better, unique, and otherwise different from the alternatives offered by your competitors.

2   Make sure they are real and specific – not general or self-serving statements like "we have the best customer service in the industry."

3   Make sure the differentiators tie back directly to the Buyer Objective Statement, and logically extend from the Offer Statement.

4   The differentiator should also be something that your buyer actually cares about. If it is different and unique but is not something of meaningful value to your buyer, then it is *not* worth adding to the value proposition. There are lots of differentiators out there. But depending on your target audience, the reality is that not all of them matter.

Here are some examples of Differentiator Statements to give you an idea of the direction you should be going in when starting to develop this section.

Example 1:

> *Our customers have achieved documented savings and efficiencies that range from 15 – 35%, and we are the only vendor that has exceeded government mandated accuracy guidelines for 5 years in a row.*

Example 2:

> *From 2000 to 2010, health plans that utilized XYZ's cost management services, solutions and technology have saved over $2.5 billion in non-network medical costs. We are the principal cost containment partners for 9 of the top 10 of the largest health insurance companies in the United States.*

Now let's get back to our own two example companies and look at the development of their differentiators. (Again, these are two organizations that I have worked with in developing their value propositions.)

Example 3: Top Line Sales

> *Our clients boast of closed contracts totaling over $100 million in new revenue due to our commitment to 'roll up our sleeves' to help your team win. We are not simply 'advice givers' – we work side-by-side with your account executives, running strategic opportunity war rooms, applying just-in-time expertise and arming them with tools and live coaching where it counts: in the field.*

Example 4: MediaConvo, Inc.

> *MediaConvo pioneered a proprietary content analysis engine to extract meaning from high volumes and diverse sources of text, a technology used by U.S. intelligence agencies for over 8 years. We are an innovator in the integration of consumer-generated media and mainstream media, offering access to the greatest breadth of content sources and analytical expertise available in the market.*

Extended Example: Top Line Sales

The Differentiator Statement for TLS came directly from the keywords brainstorm, as you can see:

Keywords	
	War room
	"roll up our sleeves"
	Not just "advice-givers"
	Live deal coaching
	Field-proven

Whereas MediaConvo, Inc. had to work really hard to nail down its Differentiator Statement (as you will see), Top Line Sales was very clear what it was from the outset. Where TLS will have more difficulty is in *quantifying* its Differentiator Statement. Particularly, it was tough to separate the features from benefits, a common challenge in service companies. It requires thinking deeply about the value that is extracted from the service. Instead of talking about what the service includes, you must reach past that and think about the *value of the outcomes* that the buyer gets from using the service.

Here is TLS's final **Differentiator**, presented in context with the Buyer Objective and the Offer Statement:

Top Line Sales Value Proposition

Buyer Objective	When was the last time each of your team members closed a seven-figure contract? Despite the best sales talent, many high potential, critical deals get whittled down or are lost completely. Large opportunities are complex and require a carefully orchestrated approach to identify, develop and win.
Offer Statement	We overcome the barriers to winning TOP Line Accounts™ whether they're worth 100K or 10M+. Top Line Sales instills the know-how into your sales organization to identify, cultivate and close strategic account opportunities through a field-proven process that includes the right tools, strategic training and live deal coaching. Our War Room service ensures that your most important account opportunities have the highest level of focus, accountability and momentum all the way through closure. This directed approach increases critical contract close ratios, and turns your sales team into strategic "Top Line" sellers.
Differentiator	Our clients boast of closed contracts totaling over $100 million in new revenue due to our commitment to 'roll up our sleeves' to help your team win. We are not simply 'advice givers' - we work side-by-side with your account executives, running strategic opportunity war rooms, applying just-in-time expertise and arming them with tools and live coaching where it counts: in the field.

Extended Example: MediaConvo

In MediaConvo's case, it was much easier. There was existing external evidence about the company and its technologies. This is often available for product companies, even product and service companies. Outside reviews are published, comparisons are made, contests are held, plus market analyst research evidence is available about certain new approaches in technology offerings. Very little of that kind of "evidence" is available for one-on-one, personalized consulting approaches that are not standardized and widely replicated through large firms. On the other hand, TLS was way ahead of MediaConvo in terms of customer testimonials and case studies that delivered specific value points quantified with real numbers. The point here is we need to be sure that our differentiators are provable. We will get deeper into how to do that in Chapter 9.

Presented below are excerpts of the competitive messaging analysis done for MediaConvo, Inc. We took our first look at this back in Chapter Four. As you review the analysis, it's painfully obvious that MediaConvo needs to ditch some language that they have been using because it is commonplace among their competitors. We identified several keywords and phrases made up of those keywords to be avoided, such as **actionable**, **insight**, and **real-time**. We also wanted to avoid overused phrases such as **market intelligence** and **market knowledge**.

When it comes to the Differentiator Statement, there is considerably less overlap. Most of the competitors' claims are empty statements offered without proof. MediaConvo has several statements that *could* be provable. If they have objective, third party proof to offer, they will be very strong on differentiators.

Remember, the proof is added to the value proposition in the next section (Chapter 9). This Differentiator Statement doesn't need to *include* the proof itself. Just be sure all the statements in this differentiator are "provable." Here's what we found among the competitor taglines. All similarities are in **BOLD** type.

MediaConvo (past version)	• Reputation Intelligence • Better Decisions. Faster
Competitors	• The Leader in Market Intelligence • The new global measurement standard in consumer-generated media • A Market Intelligence Revolution • Fearlessly seeking the reasons why • To a marketer or manufacturer this is noise. To us, it's the sound of consumer experience. • Powerful technology with human intelligence to deliver actionable brand protection and market intelligence solutions that solve everyday business problems. • Manage Risk. Leverage Opportunity • Insight Expertise Strategy

Here are examples of competitor keywords as well:

Actionable Market Knowledge	Comprehensive **real-time insight**	Market communication measurement and analysis
Understand business outcomes	Short list: Monitor, Discover, Trend, Compare, Analyze, Correlate	
360° View of Business 360° Vision	Real Time **Insight** Take **action**	Real World Business **Actionable insight**
Actionable consumer **insights**	**Insight** = Value	"always on conversations"
Listen and learn	**Insightful**	Raw data into **Actionable** Planning
Actionable insights that can drive you to your business goals		

Finally, we looked at examples of MediaConvo's and their competitors' points of differentiation and claims of advantage. MediaConvo's differentiators on this chart are the old version, before they wrote their new value proposition.

MediaConvo (past version)	• Best service in the industry – 90% client renewal • First to market with CGM/MSM solution • Thought leaders in CGM applications • Best overall accuracy: best technology paired with human analysis • Tracks interplay between MSM and CGM
Competitors	• Point of view sentiment – tone measurement • Applying marketing intelligence to business problems • Extensive backgrounds in business intelligence and analytics solutions • Defining business and marketing intelligence space • Technology leadership: federated content discovery • Content mining • ROI driven solutions • Unique methodologies • Analysts • Leader in Word of Mouth Marketing • Impartiality of our role as listener • Putting the power of information in your hands and not forcing you to engage in long-term consulting assignments • The principals have over 30 years of combined expertise and experience in developing marketing intelligence applications using natural language processing and machine learning • 8 years of experience mining and facilitating online discussion

I'm adding one more line from the MediaConvo competitive messaging scan below because it's so important to the differentiator. I called it "Focus" in my grid. Focus is about defining the primary topic or approach to the buyer's needs. The primary focus for marketing and public relations departments considering solutions in this area had to do with the two media sources that Marketing, and PR firms were most interested in tracking at this point in time: Consumer-generated Media (CGM, content generated by consumers in the form of blogs, tweets, Facebook comments and posts, etc.) and Mainstream Media (MSM, journalists and regular, standard media channels).

Focus	
CGM & MSM	MediaConvo and 2 competitors
GCM only	5 competitors
MSM only	1 competitor

MediaConvo has a first-to-market advantage in being able to track both CGM and MSM. Only two of their competitors have followed in this area. Five of them claim only CGM and one claims only MSM. We should expect the "first-to-market with the dual options" to be a prominent differentiator.

You can see from MediaConvo's differentiator for the marketing audience (Draft 4, above) that they were successful in writing an effective Differentiator Statement, using words like "pioneered," "proprietary," "innovator," and stating that what they do is "extract meaning from high volumes and diverse sources of text."

Next, let's review four drafts of the MediaConvo Differentiator Statement, written for the Marketing version shown above. It should demonstrate exactly how this statement evolved as the team worked on it.

Draft 1 Key Differentiator:

> *MediaConvo is a pioneer in the integration of CGM and MSM through its innovative technology, used by US intelligence agencies for 8 years.*

The first statement is very brief, emphasizing the first-mover advantage in the integration of CGM and MSM. Adding the key point that US intelligence agencies used this technology is a strong addition, providing a "proof of quality" to the statement. Notice that "the integration of CGM and MSM" is a feature, not a benefit. It doesn't become a benefit until MediaConvo links it to a value or outcome that is important to a buyer.

Draft 2 Key Differentiator:

> *MediaConvo is a pioneer in the integration of CGM and MSM, **offering access to the greatest breadth of content sources** and the innovative technology **to extract meaning,** a technology used by U.S intelligence agencies for 8 years.*

The first revision adds mention of "access" to the breadth of available sources and reveals that the technology used by intelligence agencies was for the purpose of extracting meaning. This revision is a big step forward because it is clearly moving from features to benefits. Benefits are "access to breadth of content sources" and "technology to extract meaning" from those content sources. Those are benefits of enormous value to the target audience. To those in Marketing or Public Relations, a big concern is having vital information missed, so the broadest access to sources is very important!

Draft 3 Key Differentiator:

> *MediaConvo pioneered the innovative technology, meeting the demands of U.S. intelligence agencies for 8 years, to extract meaning from high volumes and diverse sources of text. We are an innovator in the integration of CGM and MSM, offering access to the greatest breadth of content sources and* **analytical expertise***.*

This draft primarily tightens up the language, although it adds the concept of "analytical expertise," which is another value or benefit, not a feature.

Draft 4 Key Differentiator:

> *MediaConvo pioneered a* **proprietary content analysis engine** *to extract meaning from high volumes and diverse sources of text, used by U.S. intelligence agencies for over 8 years. We are an innovator in the integration of CGM and MSM, offering access to the greatest breadth of content sources and analytical expertise* **available in the market***.*

This final draft describes the "innovative technology" as "a proprietary content analysis engine." The language is tight, specific, original, and avoids any hint of the overused common language that was discovered in the competitive analysis. If MediaConvo can develop compelling proofs for these statements, their value proposition will look very strong.

Using a similar approach and working through a series of drafts to refine and tighten the language, will deliver a strong value proposition for you as well.

Here's what the differentiator of the MediaConvo value proposition (Marketing Version) now looks like in context with the Buyer Objective and the Offer Statement:

Value Proposition	
Customer Objective	Tuning into the voice of your market is becoming more difficult due to the millions of consumer-to-consumer conversations that are diluting the impact of your company's marketing programs. In today's Influence 2.0 world, consumers are creating their own brand dialog by blending your product messaging with their own experiences and opinions, other consumers' input, and traditional media content. Can you afford to be out of sync with your market?
Company Offer	MediaConvo, a market influence analytics company, sifts and interprets the millions of voices at the intersection of consumer-generated and traditional media. Our award-winning platform, Opus, integrates innovative technology with expert analysis to identify the people, issues and trends impacting your business—at the speed of the market.
Differentiator	MediaConvo pioneered a proprietary content analysis engine to extract meaning from high volumes and diverse sources of text, a technology used by U.S. intelligence agencies for over 8 years. We are an innovator in the integration of consumer-generated media and mainstream media, offering access to the greatest breadth of content sources and analytical expertise available in the market.

When you are satisfied with your **Differentiator Statement**, you'll be ready to move ahead to backing everything up with **Value Drivers**, **Quantification**, and **Proof**! That's what the next chapter is all about. You are now on the home stretch of building out your entire **Value Proposition Platform.**

VALUE POINTS

According to our research, buyers appreciate new value, added value, and ongoing value, but they express a preference for ongoing value. If you can bake that into your value proposition differentiator, it will go a long way to making it truly differentiated.

The key attribute of a differentiator is focusing on those "unique" aspects that a buyer will truly value. Don't know which ones they care about? Ask them!

Differentiators must be believable (not far-fetched), valuable to the buyer, specific, and provable.

Scan your competitor's tag lines, keywords, value propositions and differentiators to avoid common language that others are using, and to help you to identify gaps / opportunities that you might be able to own.

Take your statement through several revisions with input from your team before you are satisfied. Ask some valued customers what they think of it as well.

9

Backing it Up with Proof

FROM THE RESEARCH: DETAILS! DETAILS!

In Chapter 4, we learned that buyers paid attention to different areas of the value proposition at different buying stages. While it is a complex matter to track your messaging throughout all buying stages, keeping focused on the top 3 areas throughout will help you keep your "eye on the buyer" consistently as you finalize your value proposition, and then later to extend it into content and sales conversations. The top three that buyers were most interested in are "Impact on our Organization," "Relevance to a Specific Need," and "Tangible Business Benefits."

Two additional value proposition areas peak in importance during the Implementation Scenarios/Evaluations stage (3), right in the middle of the process. One is "Quantification" and one is "Address Potential Risks and Rewards."

One of the biggest weaknesses that many value propositions have is a lack of real proof to back up claims of value. Without it, your value proposition becomes just a "marketing statement" which may not have enough impact to really influence a buyer's thinking and decision making. This leaves your sales people scrambling to try and back it up – either by pestering you for case studies or testimonials at the last minute or figuring it out on their own. With either one of these outcomes, you run the risk of inconsistent messaging, and not having proof points at the time the buyer needs them.

A well-developed **Value Proposition Platform** includes three key items that provide complete back up. They are modular in nature, allowing both Marketing and Sales to pick and choose the most appropriate back-up for different scenarios and outputs. The next step you need to work on after you complete the main sections of your platform are: **Value Drivers**, **Quantification**, and objective, third-party **Proof**. You can assemble different sets for different versions of your value proposition, and your sales team can use different versions in conversation with the various buying team members with whom they will be speaking. Adding this section of elements assures consistent messaging throughout and helps "prove out" your core value proposition statement as you develop it. As you select the value drivers to extend your statements, keep in mind that if you can't quantify it in some way, then it isn't a value point that is supportable. Move on to something that has some teeth!

An area that bears additional scrutiny is the need for objective third party proof. In our research, we asked survey respondents to assign a value to all the value proposition areas. Third party proof was rated the *least* important in four of the five buying stages, and second-to-last in that fifth category. However, when we queried them about value prop weaknesses they had observed in value propositions they have considered in buying decisions, 39% of them pointed to "No proof offered" as an issue; it rated third on the list of nine weaknesses. The take-away here is that if proof is present, it is perceived as a base-line requirement that they expect to see. But leave it out, and you're treading on thin ice!

Developing Value Drivers

Now that you have worked through all three parts of your value proposition statement, you are ready to start to build out the rest of your **Value Proposition Platform**. First and foremost, it is a great test of the statements that you have developed. Can you quantify and offer proof of your claims? If not, you must go back to the drawing board. The first place to go back to is the buyer's needs and ask yourself: Have I chosen just those needs that we legitimately address? How does our offering stand up to them? What is really and truly differentiating?

The platform will give you all the supporting factors which you need to deliver a solid, consistent, and buyer-focused message across all modes of marketing and sales communications:

- Your website

- Your marketing content (brochures, fact sheets, flyers, webinars, etc.)

- Your social media content

- Your sales materials

- Sales conversations

What is a Value Driver, Anyway?

It is a set of key words that quickly highlights the most important value points that are front-of-mind for the buyer as they work through their buying process. It helps focus your messaging to center on the points that a buyer considers first in every decision around your offer category. It extends the value proposition beyond the statement itself. It forces the discipline of figuring out what ARE the key value points for your buyer? Once you've come up with these keywords, then you have a couple of tests that will help you decide if these value points really are the right ones.

Test 1: Can you quantify the value point?

Quantification can be done in a couple of ways. The first is to approximate any subjective aspect (attribute, characteristic, property) of the stated driver into numbers. It can take the form of things like statistics, actual numbers or metrics, survey results. The second method is to use hard metrics that you already have collected and use them directly to back up the point. These are real numbers or percentages that measure things like increases or decreases in factors that the buyers value. If you can't come up with quantification using either method, then how important do you think that driver really is for inclusion in your **Value Proposition Platform**? Is that value driver actually real?

Test 2: Can you prove that your offer delivers on the value point?

Proof is all about credibility. What makes it credible is when it has been validated by an objective third party. This means what someone or something OTHER than your company says about the product or service. Buyers expect you to say good things about your own offer. Most buyers take that with a grain of salt. Quantification and Proof take the "claims" of your value drivers and elevate them to real, provable points that will flesh out the value proposition in a tangible way. In effect, it "certifies" that it is real.

To create a set of value drivers, begin by answering the following question:

*What are the most important values that guide your buyer
in considering products or services in your offer category?*

Notice that the question is not about the most important features of your offer. These values should relate directly to the needs of your buyers and what is important to them.

Your product or service might have the best features in the world. It even may be the only one in the world – for now – but beware of competitors who may add it soon. The key is to identify and articulate what about that feature delivers something of value to the buyer. One way to start this section is to look at the business issues of your buyers that you have identified and the value proposition statement to pull key words out. Let's go back to our two example companies to see what they did.

Example: MediaConvo, Inc.

Business Issues		
	1	Difficult to track how marketing messages are being perceived in the social media world—too many sources and voices
	2	Content about our brand is being created by people external to our company and don't always know what they are saying
	3	Difficulty tracking multiple external blogs and twitter feeds to track how our messaging is playing out in our markets
	4	Don't have a standardized and automated way to collect mentions—very labor intensive pulling from multiple systems and individual research
	5	Creating social media metrics is very subjective—hard to manage and derive meaning
	6	Hard to access the perceptions of our brand in all our markets

Value Proposition

Buyer Objective

Tuning into the voice of your market is becoming more difficult due to the millions of consumer-to-consumer conversations that are diluting the impact of your company's marketing programs. In today's Influence 2.0 world, consumers are creating their own brand dialog by blending your product messaging with their own experiences and opinions, other consumers' input, and traditional media content. Can you afford to be out of sync with your market?

Company Offer

MediaConvo, a market influence analytics company, sifts and interprets the millions of voices at the intersection of consumer-generated and traditional media. Our award-winning platform, Opus, integrates innovative technology with expert analysis to identify the people, issues and trends impacting your business—at the speed of the market.

Differentiator	MediaConvo pioneered a proprietary content analysis engine to extract meaning from high volumes and diverse sources of text, a technology used by U.S. intelligence agencies for over 8 years. We are an innovator in the integration of consumer-generated media and mainstream media, offering access to the greatest breadth of content sources and analytical expertise available in the market.

- Breadth of information sources
- Accuracy of the information
- Timeliness of the information
- Impact on our business

- Integration of multiple sources
- Market coverage
- Relevant to our market and brand

The next step is to take this list and boil them down to one or two words. Your list now looks like this:

- Breadth
- Accuracy
- Timeliness
- Impact

- Coverage
- Relevance
- Immediacy
- Integration

The advantage that you get from boiling these down in this manner is many-fold. First, you now have a key set of topics that you can build content around – blog posts, articles, whitepapers, etc. Secondly, each of these enable sales people to conduct highly focused sales conversations on the most important aspects of the offering – without focusing entirely on features. It enables a VALUE conversation. The modularity of this approach provides consistent messaging and vital flexibility. You can lead with any one of these drivers, depending on what most interests the buyer at any given point in time. Or you can choose to zero in on a particular driver in different kinds of content. This is so much better than the typical "elevator pitch" approach to value propositions!

Example: Top Line Sales

Business Issues		
	1	Our sales results are not good enough.
	2	I don't have time to focus on strategic account development.
	3	My team lacks skills to pursue, close, expand and retain large accounts.
	4	We don't do a good job of differentiating from the competition.
	5	My team is inconsistent in landing larger deals.

Value Proposition

Customer Objective	When was the last time each of your team members closed a seven-figure contract? Despite the best sales talent, many high potential, critical deals get whittled down or are lost completely. Large opportunities are complex and require a carefully orchestrated approach to identify, develop and win.
Company Offer	We overcome the barriers to winning TOP Line Accounts™ whether they're worth 100K or 10M+. Top Line Sales instills the know-how into your sales organization to identify, cultivate and close strategic account opportunities through a field-proven process that includes, the right tools, strategic training and live deal coaching. Our War Room service ensures that your most important account opportunities have the highest level of focus, accountability and momentum all the way through closure. This directed approach increases critical contract close ratios, and turns your sales team into strategic "Top Line" sellers.

Differentiator	Our clients boast of closed contracts totaling over $100 million in new revenue due to our commitment to 'roll up our sleeves' to help your team win. We are not simply 'advice givers' - we work side-by side with your account executives, running strategic opportunity war rooms, applying just-in-time expertise and arming them with tools and live coaching where it counts: in the field.

Here are the value drivers that Top Line Sales selected:

- Larger contracts
- Improved close ratios of big deals
- Revenue stability
- Large clients will multiply value of the company

- Sales growth
- Retain and grow largest accounts
- Increasing value of business

After cutting through it, all the things that Top Line Sales buyers need are about achieving clear results: better performance in selling and growing large account deals. No specific features are important to them, unless their team can produce closed large deals and impact revenue as a result of the training, coaching and consulting that TLS delivers. The first four items on this list are for all TLS buyers while the last three are specific to owners and CEOs.

Focus on *no more* than five value drivers, as buyers won't really retain more. Of this list, narrow it down to just those value drivers that you can provide some "meat" with when you're talking about them. By meat, I mean being able to quantify the value driver in some way and then offer objective proof to support the value driver. With those two items - Quantification and Proof - the value point stays on the list. If you can't quantify it in some way, or you can't offer some form of proof, then there is no advantage to including it in your **Value Proposition Platform**.

Boiling down the value drivers this way is an excellent exercise to keep the focus on the buyer, guide key marketing messages, and serve as good talking points for Sales. Any salesperson will be happy to receive a list of key values that are important to the buyer, with a way to strengthen the conversation with data points and proof points. It's worth the extra steps to have these additional pieces to make using the value proposition clear and consistent across your marketing and sales channels.

Quantification

The next step is to build the case for the value driver to make it tangible. Using the MediaConvo, Inc. example value proposition above, if the buyer values the "Immediacy" of information about their brand, then how can we quantify the importance of that driver? It's the "show me, don't just tell me" that supports the underpinning of your overall value proposition. There are a variety of ways to quantify this. Depending on the status of your offer, whether it is new or well-established, there are multiple options for quantification.

Options for Quantification

- Data from customer results ($ or % values)

- Aggregated data from a group of customers ($ or % values)

- Statistics from an industry expert that support the intent of the value driver

- Survey or research results with attribution from an industry relevant source

- Industry or expertise award or mention for that particular value point

- Documented improvements or reductions in attributes like revenue or costs

In the case of a brand-new product or service where you do not have actual customers yet, explore what is *possible* by doing some research for supporting quantification points. Looking at outside secondary research can be very helpful. Or you can conduct your own primary research via surveys or buyer interviews. But until you do this step, your new product or service value drivers will be just ideas. It is important here to note that this must be *factual information* that can be attributed to an external third party who is talking about the substance of the value driver. It can be specifically about your product or service or be factual data about the topic. This is necessary to build credibility around the premise that your offer delivers on this value point for the buyer.

In the case of MediaConvo, Inc., they had access to two awards won by the company that were applicable to two of their value drivers. One award was used in the marketing version of the value proposition. The mere fact that actual awards categories exist for these two factors is also a good indicator that both of those value drivers are good choices to include. MediaConvo also included statistics from two published surveys, with attribution for the sources of the statistics. This approach for quantification underlines the importance of the value driver and raises the credibility factor. It tells the prospect that this is an important value driver of their decision, and here is why it is important.

Top Line Sales had access to data from both individual direct customer results, and some degree of aggregated customer data. This is really the nirvana of quantification points. There is nothing better in the eyes of a potential buyer than validated results from an existing customer. It speaks directly to what kind of an experience and outcome will be had if the buyer chooses TLS's offering.

Gathering Proof

The final piece of your **Value Proposition Platform** is providing the proof points that will support all your value messaging. This step is key in backing up all the major statements you are making about your product or service. It is the ammunition that helps solidify the offer in the eyes of the prospect or customer. It is a key tool that all salespeople need to move a buyer through the later stages of the buying process.

To make your value proposition stand out, your value drivers need to be relevant, quantified and provable. Why? Because otherwise you are just delivering "marketing speak" that may sound pretty but is not going to be believable to your audience. Buyers are sophisticated and can gather plenty of information about your offerings and their validity on their own. By providing "proof," you can shorten the sales cycle, address uncertainties early in the process, and set your offer apart from alternatives.

So, what does proof look like in the context of a value proposition? Ideally you should have one to three proof points to support each value driver and its quantification. As a product or service offering ages, you can replace weaker proof points with stronger ones—better customer testimonials, stronger case studies, perhaps more awards.

Options for Proof

- Quotes from experts
- Partner testimonials
- Market Analyst quotes & reports
- Factoids from key industry sources
- Client testimonial
- Outside research studies
- Case studies

Think of proof as an objective and unbiased opinion to support the fact that your offer delivers on the value driver. When you are looking for proof points, consider what your specific audience will see as valuable input to their decision-making process.

To get started, answer the following questions:

- Do we have customers that have agreed to give us a testimonial statement or participate in a case study that is relevant to this offering?

- Do we have partners that can provide or have provided a testimonial statement or participated in a case study?

- Which key industry groups do our audience turn to?

- Are there any industry market analysts that are talking about our product or service category?

- Are there any significant industry research studies within the past year or so that would be relevant to this offering?

Gather up the results of these questions, then evaluate which pieces of information would provide the most credible proof of the value drivers. This may take some time and some research, especially if you do not have customer or partner statements to include. You can add those later when they become available. Keep in mind that you don't want to rely on "weak" proof. Evaluate all the proof points that you gather. Focus on the one or two proof points for each value driver that are strongest and most relevant to the essence of the value driver.

In MediaConvo's case, their primary buyers (marketing department titles) were far more interested in the user-friendliness of the software, and the ability to have MediaConvo people use it for them, than they were in the technical aspects of how the software works. Nevertheless, the potential buyer's Information Technology (IT) department will be key influencers. Given that the product itself was a software platform, the marketing and public relations end users will most likely not be able to buy it if it doesn't pass muster with IT. At some point you have to offer proof for these influencers, such as MediaConvo did with the statement that the technology was used by U.S. intelligence agencies for more than eight years.

If you are creating different versions of your value proposition, you may need to augment your drivers or replace some of them with others – depending on the markets and buyers that apply to the additional versions. If you have different titles that are part of a buying team, the salespeople will need value drivers, quantification and proof points that are aimed at each key role. Some of your core value drivers will apply across buyer types, while others may be role or industry specific. The beauty of this modular approach is that you can add, move, or vary each piece to serve the buyer you are targeting – and still adhere to the integrity and consistency of the value proposition message you are trying to get across.

Extended Example: Top Line Sales

Top Line Sales had an advantage in gathering proof points: they had delivered the same services for several years' time. Customer case studies were the most useful elements to quantify TLS's claims. It may take a year or two or more before a TLS client has a big financial return to show for its investment. When it does, however, the results can be huge. This kind of ROI simply doesn't lend itself to a simple quote. Therefore, the **Value Proposition Platform** itself refers to three case studies, or stories, that TLS was able to use on its website, in sales calls, marketing literature, and other messaging.

These are the value drivers included in the Top Line Sales **Value Proposition Platform** and the quantification references:

Value Drivers	Quantification
Improved close ratios of big deals	Fortune 50 Manufacturing Client Case: $25m deal, largest in company that year
Sales growth	High Tech Client Case: Six-fold increase in 'million-dollar' deals over the past year alone.
Retain and grow largest accounts	Healthcare Insurance Client Case: Retained multi-million $ client through RFP Rebid

Here is the case example that supports the first value driver: "Improved close rations of big deals."

Manufacturing Client:

I want to share an inspirational story that underscores the importance of the pre-strategy SWOT as a foundational element of the TOP·Line Account™ strategy war room. I'll never forget a strategy meeting with one of my clients, a Fortune 50 technology company, who was trying to determine if they should go after an opportunity or not. They weren't sure they could compete, and the VP of Sales asked me to join the session to help them decide. After laying out all the elements, we decided they had a shot. I continued to work with the team ensuring that we had a strategic approach to every step of the sales process. A year and a half later, they won the deal, worth $20M, the largest contract of its kind in the company that year.

This is the case example supporting the second value driver: Sales Growth.

High Technology Client:

The below quotes are paraphrased from two Global Account Managers (GAM's) who are with a global, fast growing technology company headquartered in the Bay Area. I worked with them to customize and instill an overlay to their sales process focusing on the development of top opportunities. This was shared during their global sales kick off meeting in New Orleans, January 2015.

The first Global Account Manager says, '*War room strategy planning highlights what you don't know and need to know to be successful.*'

The second Global Account Manager says, '*The war room approach forces you to think through tactics and strategies... It enables you to prioritize and align effectively and it brings clarity to lengthy and complex sales cycles.*'

This particular company has seen a six-fold increase in 'million dollar' deals over the past year alone!

And finally, this story supports the third value driver: Retain and Grow Largest Accounts.

Healthcare Insurance Client:

Here's a sales scenario you've all heard before. I was helping a healthcare insurance client whose largest customer issued an RFP which included all the services they were providing. They were very concerned about the impact to their business in light of the competitive bid process. As we all know, anything can happen during an RFP. We held a war room meeting to determine what it would take to retain the account. We started with a complete dossier on each competitor. From that analysis, we were able to hone in on our 'win themes' or those areas of differentiation for my client which also put the lead competitor at a disadvantage. We made sure that each answer in their RFP response emphasized at least one win theme, and also included an example or evidence to further solidify our points. This was a very different approach from their normal bid responses which were professional but generic. The win themes carried through in the presentation stage and also during all interactions with the customer. My client won the RFP, retained their customer, worth millions to the organization, and continues to enjoy significant business from that customer today.

What you can learn from the TLS examples is that you don't need to make your proof points fit the actual format used in my **Value Proposition Platform** template. The template is a "cheat sheet" to simplify internal communication, and to help you gather and review all the pieces of the platform to ensure that they all fit well together. Add additional materials in a variety of ways by gathering the best stories, cases, quotes and other evidence that you can find. You may want to consider putting all the additional value proposition materials – along with the completed **Value Proposition Platform** template – in a single repository to make it easier to use across a variety of media (web, email, tweets, blogs, presentations, webinars, videos, podcasts). This greatly simplifies the sharing of the modular pieces of your value proposition to everyone on your internal marketing and sales teams, and with your target audiences.

The other take-away here is that even though TLS does not disclose the client names, there is no doubt that these are genuine examples. They have an infallible ring of truth. And they really can't be expressed in a sound bite or short quotation.

TLS also had to work at requesting formal testimonials (quotations) in a format that is usable for a **Value Proposition Platform**. The same thing may occur with you. When you ask clients for a testimonial, tell them what you need.

- One or two sentences

- Specific results attributable to your company's work with them

- Focused on one or more value drivers

You can write the testimonial for them, send it as a draft, and say, "Is this acceptable? Would you edit this as you see fit? May I use this on my website (in my sales literature, etc.)?" You should also ask if you can use their name, title, and their company logo if it is recognizable. If not, can you use their quote, attributed to "VP of Sales, National Healthcare Company?" Many large companies have serious restrictions about employee quotations, and the request may have to pass through their communications department, and often the legal department as well. My point is, don't leave testimonials to chance when what you need is quantifiable evidence. Ask your customers for exactly what you need. They will be happy to help you out, and it will save them time and energy if you give them a draft that they can review and edit as needed. You are much more likely to get one if you don't make them start with a blank piece of paper!

The other work that TLS did was to write the case studies. Top Line Sales simply did not have enough short, 1-2-line quotations specifically dedicated to the value drivers that they had selected. After making new requests to their existing selection, they had an ample collection. Many are visible throughout TLS' website today.

Top Line Sales now has a compelling selection of material to back up its value proposition. See how the proof lines up with each value driver and quantification below:

Value Drivers	Quantification	Proof
Improved close ratios of big deals	Fortune 50 Manufacturing Client Case $25m deal, largest in company that year	"Because of our relationship with Top Line Sales, sales management now has a clear line of sight between sales goals and revenue results." Sandy Barnes, Cameron Design Group
Sales growth	High Tech Client Case: six-fold increase in 'million-dollar' deals over the past year alone.	"This approach has translated into greater consistency, meaning fewer valleys and higher peaks in the volume of closed sales." Mark M. Fallon, President & CEO, The Berkshire Company
Retain and grow largest accounts	Healthcare Insurance Client Case: Retained multi-million $ client through RFP Rebid	"The investment will have far reaching returns with improving our sales conversation, consistently understanding the customer's point of view, improved confidence of our sales people and retention of our most important and strategic customers." Jeni Billups, Senior VP, Sales & Marketing, Oregon Freeze Dry

Now let's look at a completely different set of back-up materials that MediaConvo, Inc. developed for their **Value Proposition Platform**.

Extended Example: MediaConvo, Inc.

One of MediaConvo's challenges was that they didn't have many recent customer testimonials, and no actual case studies had been written. The company was founded by a team of technologists who spent much of their investment dollars on product improvements, and very little on marketing. Like many technology companies, the focus was on sales only – leaving salespeople to figure out the messaging on their own.

To start, we decided to focus on identifying the most credible voices in their buyers' industries that could potentially provide the proof points to back up the value of their offering. To reiterate an earlier point, if you don't have testimonials and case studies to use (as in the case of a new offering), then focus on the industry experts and statistics as a way to start. While MediaConvo had customers, they didn't have enough content from them to cover all the proof points needed. Given the amount of time it takes to get permission, to craft statements and case studies, and then get customer approval (marketing, communications, legal), it made sense in the short term to look at *other* ways to address the need for proof.

The examples MediaConvo used as proof points for the Public Relations version of their value proposition included a quote from one of the largest PR agencies in the U.S. (a key target for this offer). The quote sited some industry research as part of their statement which was a double benefit that made the proof statement even more solid. MediaConvo also did have a client quote as the second proof point. This is always the best proof to offer when it is available. Nothing will be as effective as what your current customers say about you. If you don't have any, or enough of them to cover your entire set of value drivers, you can always add them over time as you are able to get approved quotes or case studies. In the meantime, third party proof points are a solid alternative and hold weight with buyers as well. The final proof point MediaConvo used comes from a major industry association which the target audience turned to for information, innovation, and recommendations. This set of proof points delivered a 1-2-3 punch!

This is how MediaConvo ultimately developed its list of value drivers and the statements of quantification and proof that they decided on for each one. They went through four stages of revision! Sometimes it can take that long – depending on the complexity of your offering, and the variety of value drivers you are considering.

During the revision process, MediaConvo considered nine value drivers. The list shows in parentheses how many editorial rounds each driver was considered for. This demonstrates the overall process of consideration and validation needed to have a value driver make it to the final **Value Proposition Platform**.

• Accuracy (2 rounds)	• Innovation (4)
• Immediacy (4)	• Service (4)
• Relevancy (4)	• Breadth (2)
• Meaning (4)	• Rigor (1)
• Impact (4)	

The first draft consisted of five of these value drivers, with the drivers of "Accuracy," "Immediacy," "Rigor," and "Service" having been eliminated in the first round. Essentially the team felt these were the top drivers. The test was going to be discovering what options they had for quantification, and what proof they had to back it up.

Presented below are a couple of views of the revision process. While there were many rounds, it's instructive to see where they started and a bit of how they got to their final set of completed drivers.

First Draft—MediaConvo Value Drivers, Quantification, and Proof

As the process continues, figuring out the best mix of drivers is one of consideration and testing. Do we have proof that backs up the value driver? Do the quantification and proof points make sense together? How do they stack up against the other options we have for drivers?

Here's the second draft, after a round of revisions. Significant changes are highlighted in gray.

Value Delivered	Quantification	Proof (Quotes)
Breadth	Combines an advanced information extraction engine covering: • 200,000 local, regional and international media outlets • Over 30 countries and 13 languages • Approx. 24 million blogs in a 24/7 real-time environment • Supplemented by message boards, Usenet newsgroups, and online opinion/review sites	Verisign: "As the media world, branding and marketing change so rapidly because more information is available to more people in different formats, we have to stay on top of it, and MediaConvo is providing us with that opportunity."
Meaning	Expert human interpretation delivered by a team of media and brand experts, grammarians and computational linguists.	TRW Automotive: "Simplified information gathering by organizing clippings in a meaningful and systematic way – while uncovering trends and relationships that are meaningful to our business."

Value Delivered	Quantification	Proof (Quotes)
Rigor	Best New Measurement Technology of 2005 awarded by The Measurement Standard	Larry Weber, formerly of Weber Shandwick "MediaConvo is delivering on its promise to provide the measurement, strategic assessment and reporting tools all marketing professionals need, designed for the way they work."
Immediacy	"Best of Show" - 2005 Massachusetts Innovation Technology Exchange, for Best Use of Technology and Applied Technology - for delivering immediate market intelligence.	Fleishman Hillard: "Allows our PR teams to dynamically adjust campaigns based on what is happening now – not what happened three months ago."
Relevancy	KMWorld's Top 100 Companies that Matter in Knowledge Management for "Customer-driven agile innovation"	KMWorld "MediaConvo is offering innovative market intelligence solutions that allow its clients to accurately measure and analyze media coverage, market leadership and corporate reputation in real-time."
Impact	A Pew study shows that 44% of online users have created content by creating or commenting on a blog, posting to an online discussion group, creating a web site, posting to a site, or sharing photos or other files online.	Brodeur Worldwide: "Helped a small Canadian software company identify aggressive advertising attacks from larger American rivals and craft an effective response. It's an element used in near real time to drive what we call rapid response."

Value Delivered	Quantification	Proof (Quotes)
Innovation	Named a BlogOn 2005's Social Media Innovator at the BlogOn 2005 Social Media Summit	Alcatel: "The physical clip book really doesn't apply when people are all over the world or all over the country...It's not always quantity; it's quality of coverage that's important. It's nice to have something that depicts both."

One of the first changes MediaConvo made was to remove "Accuracy" from the value driver list. It was replaced by "Breadth" as a new driver. Its quantification was extracted from another driver - "Meaning" - and it referred to the range of sources available in their platform. This point was to emphasize the amount of media content sources that MediaConvo provided access to via its platform. A key buyer issue for both the marketing and public relations sectors is that they need to be sure relevant content out there is not missed, so any offering that can deliver the greatest "breadth" of sources is extremely valuable. For that reason, it made sense to move this value driver to the top of the list. MediaConvo also took the last piece of the original quantification and retained it for "Meaning" as a separate driver. This spoke to the use of human experts to supplement the data searches conducted by the software platform. Having a set of eyes to make sure that all the citations that come from the platform are relevant is important enough to call it out separately. It follows "Breadth" as a natural next value. Why? As a marketer, I want the greatest number of sources, but I also want to be certain that everything cited is meaningful to my search. The key point here is that MediaConvo went back to the business needs of their target buyers to really think through which drivers would speak most directly to the value points they would be focused on in considering an offering like this.

Three other additions were made to the list of drivers: "Rigor," Immediacy," and" Service". The first speaks to having the most current and up-to-date content available – a big issue when it comes to the "immediate" nature of consumer-generated media (i.e. social media). Their buyers don't want "old" citations – they need more of a just-in-time approach. Service was added because they want to stress the important point that their renewal rate is high, making the case that this is a direct result of the level of service they deliver along with the software platform. It also spoke to how well the platform delivers in terms of its claims. If 90% of their customers renew, then they clearly are getting value out of the product. Finding a solid service proof point or quote was noted as needing to be addressed.

The Next Revision: Version 3

Value Delivered	Quantification	Proof
Accuracy	Best New Measurement Technology of 2005 awarded by The Measurement Standard	Verisign: "Gives us much greater detail in terms of our coverage."
Immediacy	"Best of Show" - 2005 Massachusetts Innovation Technology Exchange, for Best Use of Technology and Applied Technology - for delivering immediate market intelligence.	Fleishman Hillard: "Allows our PR teams to dynamically adjust campaigns based on what is happening now – not what happened three months ago."

Value Delivered	Quantification	Proof
Relevancy	66 percent of surveyed companies are operating under the assumption that "the effect of consumer-created content on brands will greatly increase over the next 12 months." Source: Jupiter Research	Lexis-Nexis: "What's exciting about this development is that it provides a new way of putting information into context."
Meaning	MediaConvo's platform combines brand intelligence and expert analysis with Natural Language Processing (NLP) technology's knowledge of sentence structure, including verb tense, modifiers, descriptors, and advanced grammars and lexicons that can pick up variations of a message. Outcomes include tracking issues, quantifying tonality, delivering insights and exposing competitive opportunities in the marketplace.	TRW Automotive: "Simplified information gathering by organizing clippings in a meaningful and systematic way – while uncovering trends and relationships that are meaningful to our business."
Impact	A Pew study shows that 44% of online users have created content by creating or commenting on a blog, posting to an online discussion group, creating a web site, posting to a site, or sharing photos or other files online.	Brodeur Worldwide: "Helped a small Canadian software company identify aggressive advertising attacks from larger American rivals and craft an effective response. It's an element used in near real time to drive what we call rapid response."

It became clear in ongoing editorial discussions that "accuracy" really is an important aspect in terms of output of the software; AND the fact that MediaConvo received an award for it totally validates the importance of the value point. The fact that an outside organization runs awards on this point makes it clear that this is something all buyers need to pay attention to. The decision was made to trade "Breadth" for "Accuracy". Why not keep both? Part of this work is trying to keep to a core set of value drivers. They could have included all the nine drivers they had brainstormed, but it was highly unlikely that any buyer would care or pay attention to that many. Here, less is definitely more. Just because we have nine drivers *does not mean* all of them really matter to the buyer – even if they matter to MediaConvo, Inc. You'll notice that various other sections (highlighted in grey) continued to change.

Throughout this process, we conducted several internal reviews with stakeholders: Product Development, IT Engineering, Marketing, and Sales. The goal is to balance the inputs to come up with a solid set of drivers that can be reviewed with MediaConvo customers for the final input. The customer view is the most important, and we conducted a set of interviews with existing MediaConvo customers to review the entire value platform. Based on their input, the final set of drivers, quantification and proof is presented below.

Final Revision: Version Four

Value Delivered	Quantification	Proof
Innovation	Named a BlogOn 2005's Social Media Innovator at the BlogOn 2005 Social Media Summit	Alcatel: "The physical clip book really doesn't apply when people are all over the world or all over the country...It's not always quantity; it's quality of coverage that's important. It's nice to have something that depicts both."
Breadth	Combines an advanced information extraction engine to locate the most critical sources from over: • 200,000 local, regional and international media outlets • 30+ countries and 13 languages • Approx. 26 million blogs in a 24/7 real-time environment • Supplemented by message boards, • Usenet newsgroups, and online opinion/review sites	Moreover Technologies: "Weblogs have become an indispensable part of the analysis of market trends and opinion. Because blogs both break news stories and add additional context and thoughtful discussion to stories from more traditional media sources, monitoring their output is essential to successful marketing efforts."

Value Delivered	Quantification	Proof
Meaning	MediaConvo's platform combines brand intelligence and expert analysis with Natural Language Processing (NLP) technology's knowledge of sentence structure. Outcomes include tracking issues, quantifying tonality, delivering insights and exposing competitive opportunities in the marketplace.	TRW Automotive: "Simplified information gathering by organizing clippings in a meaningful and systematic way – while uncovering trends and relationships that are meaningful to our business."
Immediacy	"Best of Show" - 2005 Massachusetts Innovation Technology Exchange, for Best Use of Technology and Applied Technology - for delivering immediate market intelligence.	Fleishman Hillard: "Allows our PR teams to dynamically adjust campaigns based on what is happening now – not what happened three months ago."
Impact	In a survey of the attitudes toward blogs, 77% of the respondents thought the regularly updated journals were a useful way to get insights into the products and services they should buy. Source: BBC Report	Brodeur Worldwide: "Helped a small Canadian software company identify aggressive advertising attacks from larger American rivals and craft an effective response. It's an element used in near real time to drive what we call rapid response"

The final version traded out "Accuracy" for "Breadth." It was noted as of primary importance by the customers with whom we spoke. While they agreed that accuracy was important, the customers felt that it is a *baseline expectation* to even be in the business. What really was more front-of-mind for them was having the widest coverage of sources possible to reduce the risk of missing important media mentions – whether they are mainstream media or consumer-generated media. The bigger risk was definitely seen as the CGM content.

MediaConvo settled on five strong value drivers backed up with quantitative statements and statements of proof from objective third party sources. This gives them a lot of flexibility for positioning of the product/service in a variety of ways, and options to pick and choose from for the two versions of the value proposition. For sales conversations, it is ideal, giving a core set of topics to roll out throughout the buyer's journey with all the selling points and back-up that any salesperson needs.

A Final Checkpoint

Before going any further with your value proposition, ask key internal audiences and key customers to take a close look and provide feedback. Even if you believe that it clearly reflects the voice and thinking of your buyer, you could be wrong! Take advantage of one more chance to validate your choices, and one more opportunity to bring your colleagues and customers closer by asking for and valuing their opinions! Consider doing an internal launch of the **Value Proposition Platform** before you start to embed it in content and roll it out to your buyer audience. It is crucial that everyone in your organization understand what the messaging means and how it ties to the buyer experience. At MediaConvo, it was rolled out at a company meeting. After the presentation, discussion and Q&A, a recently hired salesperson shared with the CMO that this was the first company she had worked with that gave the team such a comprehensive and clear set of messages for sales conversations. Further validation was given when the company was acquired several years later by another much larger player in their market space. MediaConvo's value proposition was cited as being a key factor in their looking at the company as a potential acquisition. Another buyer won over!

In the next chapter, we'll examine ways of integrating your value proposition throughout your sales and marketing activities, and some additional ideas on how to roll it out across your company.

VALUE POINTS

The Value Drivers, Quantification, and Proof Statements that back up your value proposition are critical to meeting the needs and interests of various buyers and to insure focus on what buyers need at different stages of the buyer's journey.

This final section of your **Value Proposition Platform** provides a set of topics you can use to create extended messaging for your website, marketing content, social media content, and sales materials.

Value Drivers are the most important value points that are top-of-mind with your buyer when considering products or services in your offer category.

Quantification involves data, statistics, survey / research results from a relevant source, awards, expert research or evaluations, or improvements / reductions in attributes like revenue or costs.

Proof consists of quotes from experts, testimonials from clients or partners, market analyst quotes or reports, outside research studies, case studies, facts from industry sources, or other evidence from objective third party sources.

10

Putting Your Value Proposition into Play

FROM THE RESEARCH: VERSIONS!

Throughout the research study, we have seen evidence that you will most likely need multiple versions of your value propositions. I'll remind you of the key reasons:

- Above all, value propositions must be relevant to the needs and interests of the buyers.

- Value propositions must be aligned with the interests and needs of a variety of buyers, titles, focus areas (business, technical and financial impact), and industries.

- Some of the differences among buyers are more important for their positive impact, others for their negative effect.

Once you have developed the primary value proposition, you should consider if there are differences that need to be reflected in any additional industries you may be targeting. Are you considering entirely different sectors and market segments? What are the different job titles within a single customer company, and how do their needs differ if they sit on the decision team for your offering?

For example, selling into a B2B market is quite different than selling into the public sector or government market. Your value proposition may need to be customized to address different business needs or different titles / roles. For this reason, versioning by industry vertical, or by different titles / roles may be necessary. In the MediaConvo example, we took the primary version (which was a Corporate version that we have not shared in this book) and created other versions of the value proposition that focused on different groupings of titles/roles. We shared two of them with you in these pages. The first was aimed at marketing titles in corporate and product marketing departments. The second version was aimed at public relations departments and public relations agencies. While the core message was similar, the business needs and some of the language was different – and versioning the value proposition assured relevancy to these two different audience targets.

Creating different versions is about honing the Buyer Objective Statement to address the specific business needs of that industry or title / role more specifically. The Offer Statement in most instances will continue to work in its original format. You may also be able to use the same Differentiator as well. You can best determine if there is a need to make any adjustments when and if there are any material differences in the primary needs of that industry or target. When you get to the Value Drivers, Quantification, and Proof, assess the need to make any changes, deletions, or additions, to ensure these supporting points directly address the additional vertical industry as well as any new titles you may have added. As always, it depends on what you sell, where you sell it, and to whom you sell it. Always go back to your target audience's business needs and you can't go wrong. Make it about them, and in the case of different audiences, prepare versions of your Buyer Objective Statements and/or Value Drivers so it speaks directly to each key audience.

In the case of MediaConvo, they developed four versions of their value proposition: a corporate version, a marketing department version, a public relations department or agency version and a customer satisfaction version. The primary change across these four types was in the Buyer Objective section. There were also variations in the value driver section as well – either listing them in a different order of priority or swapping in a new one for an existing one, as needed, to drive home the right value points.

The highest-level version, and the one that will be the most prominent on the website, is the Corporate Version.

Corporate – Buyer Objective

> *The dynamic of influencing consumers has shifted. In today's Influence 2.0 world, consumers are creating their own brand dialogue by blending your product messaging with their own experiences and opinions, other consumers' input, and traditional media content. Can you afford to be out of sync with your market?*

Public Relations – Buyer Objective

> *The voice of the media has become fragmented across a complex array of sources with the addition of blogs, message boards, Usenet newsgroups, and online opinion/review sites. In today's Influence 2.0*

world, these sources become entwined as journalists pick up story ideas from bloggers and bloggers remark on traditional media and corporate content. This new brand dialogue demands an understanding of the consumer experience beyond traditional tracking of key message pickup. Can you afford to be out of sync with your market?

Marketing – Buyer Objective

Tuning into the voice of your market is becoming more difficult due to the millions of consumer-to-consumer conversations that are diluting the impact of your company's marketing programs. In today's Influence 2.0 world, consumers are creating their own brand dialogue by blending your product messaging with their own experiences and opinions, other consumers' input, and traditional media content. Can you afford to be out of sync with your market?

Customer Satisfaction – Buyer Objective

The voice of the customer praises, demands, instructs and leads other consumers into making decisions for or against your products and services. Beyond communicating with a company's customer service or consumer affairs departments, customer concerns are also voiced on blogs, message boards, Usenet newsgroups, and online opinion/review sites. In today's Influence 2.0 world, these experiences and opinions are added to your brand messaging, and traditional media content to become part of the consumer-controlled brand dialogue. Can you afford to be out of sync with your market?

As you can see from these different versions, the core message is still consistent through-out all of them. Where the changes occur is in the opening of each where the concerns of the different audience types are clearly addressed. A good next step once you have these Buyer Objective Statements is to see if all the original set of drivers are appropri-ate for each audience. Does the order need to change because one driver may be more important or primary to one audience versus another? Or do you need to remove a driver and replace it (along with its quantification and proof points) and substitute in or add another relevant driver for that audience? The good news is that the **Value Proposition Platform** is designed to be modular. You can change, add, replace as needed dependent on the needs of your different buyers. So, you do not have to ever start with a blank sheet of paper when you are addressing a new market or title/role.

Your Value Props are Done – Now What?

It's time to get busy and use the new messaging represented by your **Value Proposition Platform** and start to plan how it is going to be integrated and used in both your marketing and sales content and activities. Below are some highlights of the information we used to do an "internal" launch of the new **Value Proposition Platform** to MediaConvo staff. At a minimum, an internal launch should include all of Marketing and Sales. It's smart to go one step further and include all prospect or customer-facing personnel, as well. Everyone who has occasion to interact with a prospect or customer should understand how the organization is presenting itself to its buyers. In the case of MediaConvo, they opted to do an internal roll-out to the entire company.

Here's how MediaConvo introduced each of the four value proposition versions to their staff. The roll-out included the following topics:

- Why new value propositions and messaging

- How the value propositions were developed

- Value proposition primer

    - Purpose & definitions

    - Types of value propositions

    - Positioning statements

- Competitive landscape – messaging

- MediaConvo value proposition hierarchy

- New value propositions – all versions

- New tag line and its meaning

- Using value propositions and positioning statements

- Putting the value proposition platform into play

The goal here is to make sure everyone understands the new message – from its inception (why new messaging), its development (how and who), the outcome (the platform itself), and how to use it. As you review it, you will notice that some of the highlights presented here "extends" the one-page **Value Proposition Platform** document with additional content and messaging. The platform template serves as a messaging foundation, as well as a cheat sheet, to go back to whenever anyone in the organization is creating content. This helps the message stay consistent across all methods of marketing and sales communications. For someone unfamiliar with how this template works, it is helpful to extend it into more of a story, and then provide insights into how it will be used.

MediaConvo Corporate Value Proposition

Buyer Objective

The dynamic of influencing consumers has shifted. In today's Influence 2.0 world, consumers are creating their own brand dialogue by blending your product messaging with their own experiences and opinions, other consumers' input, and traditional media content. Can you afford to be out of sync with your market?

MediaConvo Offer:

MediaConvo, **a market influence analytics** company, sifts and interprets the millions of voices at the intersection of consumer-generated and traditional media. Our award-winning platform, Opus, integrates innovative technology with expert analysis to identify the people, issues and trends impacting your business—at the speed of the market.

MediaConvo Differentiator:

MediaConvo pioneered a proprietary content analysis engine to extract meaning from high volumes and diverse sources of text, a technology used by U.S. intelligence agencies for over 8 years. We are an innovator in the integration of consumer-generated media and traditional media, offering access to the greatest breadth of content sources and analytical expertise available in the market.

Understanding the terminology "Market Influence Analytics"

- MediaConvo's unique position is to differentiate ourselves in the industry

- Competitors talk about what they do: "media measurement" or "consumer-generated media tracking"

- Our message focuses on the customer's need to measure the influence they are having on their audience through their marketing and public relations.

- **Market Influence Analytics** gives clients the information they need to understand the changing landscape:

- The power of influence has shifted away from companies and to the consumer

- Mainstream media doesn't have the influence it once had

- Consumers are connecting directly to each other and sharing their opinions, experiences and recommendations and influencing their purchase decisions

- Traditional media and consumer-generated media interact and influence each other, amplifying the impact of each other

Positioning Statement – Corporate Value Proposition

For (target customer)	For market-facing professionals who: • Worry about the impact of consumer-generated media on their brands • Require timely insight on consumer opinions • Concerned about threats to corporate reputation • Must demonstrate measurable success to senior executives
Who Need	• Who need to harness the new dynamic of influencing consumers by plugging into the intersection of consumer-generated media and traditional media to track, measure, and understand consumer-controlled brand dialogues.
The (solution) is in a (category)	• MediaConvo, a market influence analytics company, sifts and interprets the millions of voices at the intersection of consumer-generated and traditional media. Our award-winning Platform, Opus, integrates innovative technology with expert analysis to identify the relevant points of influence impacting your business— at the speed of the market.

That delivers (compelling value)	Breadth: Combines an advanced information extraction engine to locate the most critical sources from over:
	• Over 26 million blogs in a 24/7 real-time environment
	• Supplemented by message boards, Usenet newsgroups, and online opinion/review sites
	• 200,000 local, regional and international media outlets
	• 30+ countries and 13 languages
	Relevance: The importance of consumer online activity has been steadily increasing. A survey conducted by Jupiter Research revealed: "66 percent of surveyed companies are operating under the assumption that "the effect of consumer-created content on brands will greatly increase over the next 12 months."
	Meaning: MediaConvo's platform combines brand intelligence and expert analysis with Natural Language Processing (NLP) technology's knowledge of sentence structure. Outcomes include tracking issues, quantifying tonality, delivering insights and exposing competitive opportunities in the marketplace.
Unlike (primary competitors)	• Unlike companies who offer access only to consumer-generated media, like Competitor C and Competitor B, or PR measurement firms like Competitor D.
Our solution (primary differentiation)	• MediaConvo pioneered a proprietary content analysis engine to extract meaning from high volumes and diverse sources of text, a technology used by U.S. intelligence agencies for over 8 years. We are an innovator in the integration of consumer-generated media and traditional media, offering access to the greatest breadth of content sources and analytical expertise available in the market.

Now their story is one that everyone can understand, and everyone can tell! **Positioning Statements** like the one above was created for each version of the value proposition (Corporate, Marketing, Public Relations, and Customer Satisfaction).

Using Your Value Proposition

Your new value proposition can become the basis for an upgrade of all your sales and marketing materials. Here's an inventory of how MediaConvo planned to use its four versions:

Refined Company Message

Customer Challenge / MedicaConvo Offer / Differentiators
Value Proposition, Positioning, Brand Essence
Company Tagline

New Marketing & Sales Materials

Graphic design refresh, New Images, Content & Formats

Website	Sales Sheets	Presentations	Whitepapers & Reports	Trade Show Booths
• PR	• PR	• PR	• PR	• PR
•Marketing	•Marketing	•Marketing	•Marketing	•Marketing
•Customer Service	•Customer Service	•Customer Service	•Customer Service	•Customer Service

Another important consideration is reviewing the versions you have created and seeing how you might customize them for different industries. MediaConvo decided their versions were going to be *role specific* (Marketing, Public Relations, etc.) Some organizations prefer to start with *industry versions* as the focus. Either way, you can take the platform that you have and extend the messaging in different ways.

For example, MediaConvo served twelve industries. If they were especially strong in two or three industries, or if they wanted to make inroads into specific industries, they could develop new value proposition versions and messaging for those specific industries. Or they could adjust their positioning statement to have a vertical industry slant. Healthcare, pharmaceutical, insurance and financial services, being highly regulated, would be good places to start. There are options in considering how you are going to take your value proposition and extend it into messaging. The three primary options are as follows:

Industry Messaging	Customizing the value proposition to address the business needs of industry-specific roles and titles. This makes your core message even more relevant for buyers in that industry.
Product / Service Messaging	Here is where you get to talk about all your product or service's features and benefits. You should be weaving in the value proposition components into your product and service marketing collateral. The combination of a buyer-focused value proposition integrated with product and service messaging is much more powerful.
Sales Messaging	Sales people need messaging served up to them in a way that makes it easy for them to conduct conversations. So, you can pull from your Value Proposition Platform to create "killer questions," and create positioning statements for each specific decision-making role, and embed the value drivers, quantification and proof points into sales presentations, and sales prompters.

Company Tagline

We know that a value proposition is *not* a tagline. But you do need a tagline, because once you have a new value proposition, your existing tagline will likely be obsolete. That was the case for MediaConvo. They had a hard time coming up with a tagline! In fact, their tagline turned out to be a very new concept when it was launched back in 2006 – so new that it required quite a bit of explaining! Here's a list of taglines they considered:

Draft Taglines

1 Market Influence Analytics

2 Market Analytics at Media Speed

3 Deciphering the new Brand Dialogue

4 Pinpoint the Voice of Your Market

5 The New Dynamic of Consumer Influence

6 Where Media Influences Action

7 Tune in to the Voice of the Market

8 Extracting Meaning. Delivering Impact.

9 Real-time Access to Market Influence

10 Engaging the Voice of the Market

11 Conversations in Context

12 The Intersection of Consumer-Generated and Mainstream Media

13 Media² — CGM x MSM = Market Impact

14 Harness the New Media Dynamic

15 Join the Media Remix Culture

16 Media Remix - Unplugged

17 Breadth Accuracy Impact

18 Listen. Understand. Act.

19 Listen. Measure. Protect.

20 Meaning. Influence. Action.

You can see they were struggling with language and emphasis! You can start this process by brainstorming as many ideas as you can think of. This is a great place to start, but don't do it in a vacuum. By that I mean the ideas should be extracted and be connected to the messaging in your **Value Proposition Platform**. That guarantees a fit when you get done.

In the next revision, they rank-ordered their favorites. In addition, they also created some new ones.

1 Market Influence Analytics

2 The New Dynamic of Consumer Influence (word "consumer" is an issue)

3 Extract Meaning. Harness Influence.

4 Real-time Access to Market Influence

5 Engaging the Voice of the Market

6 $Media^2$ — CGM x MSM = Influence 2.0

7 "Impact" to "Influence 2.0"

8 Influence 2.0

- Customer Engagement 2.0

- Engagement 2.0

- Customer Influence 2.0

- Harness the New Media Dynamic

9 Meaning Influence Action

10 Harnessing the New Dynamic of Consumer Influence

- Harnessing Market Influence and Action (Impact)

- From Market Influence to Action

- Market Influence to Impact

- Influence to Impact

At some point during the process, they came up with the phrase "Influence 2.0," which wasn't even on their original list. Then they played with iterations of 2.0, finally settling on "Influence 2.0" as the tagline.

A quick word of context is in order here. Today, Influence 2.0 is not a novel idea, and the concept of influence marketing is now deeply entrenched. But in 2006, it was still in the invention stage. MediaConvo's Chief Marketing Officer was involved in the Influence 2.0 Wiki Project, Chapter One entitled "The Dawn of the Age of Influence." It was all about how Web 2.0 was changing the marketing and public relations business. They had not even fully converted the word "weblog" to "blog" at that point! This is an important point because you may be lucky enough to capture something truly new, completely unique, in your own value proposition work. Realize this now: it won't last forever – just as no product or service innovation lasts forever. But grab it and use it while you can.

If your organization creates a new term or a new idea, you have a big decision to make. Do you risk going with it? Do you have the courage that MediaConvo exhibited to build it prominently into their customer objective statements, trusting their team to turn it into industry language of which they claimed ownership? They decided to go for it, and that phrase did become a key term in their market for a significant period.

Having made that decision (another reason why you MUST have high-level support for this project!), here's how MediaConvo rolled the tagline out to the rest of the company:

Company Tagline: INFLUENCE 2.0

Influence 1.0	Influence 2.0
• Companies influence consumers with finely-crafted media messages	• Consumers take control and influence how the message appears to others
• One-way communication at the consumer	• Active consumer discussion and debate with each other
• Limited consumer reach "around the water cooler"	• Limitless reach to many others on the web with blogs and social media
• Stories represent a single point of view	• Stories harness the collective intelligence of the community
• Publications quickly archive stories, or charge a fee to a small group	• Content lives on blogs forever – free of charge to all
• Companies have the greatest influence over traditional media stories	• Journalists actively review social media to identify stories

Elevator Speech

Now because you have the benefit of a full messaging platform, the elevator speech comes directly from the company offer. It's a simple restatement, as the MediaConvo example below illustrates.

> *MediaConvo is a market influence analytics company, helping marketing and PR professionals uncover new business opportunities and identify threats to corporate reputation by sifting and interpreting both consumer-generated media (CGM) and mainstream media (MSM), at the speed of the market.*

Sales and Marketing Content

Let's go down a level further and look at the different areas of marketing and sales content into which you will need to integrate your value proposition messaging. You can customize this chart to reflect the types of content that you typically produce to engage your customers and prospects, and it will help you visualize how the value proposition can feed into your overall marketing and sales communication plans.

Integrating the Value Proposition Platform

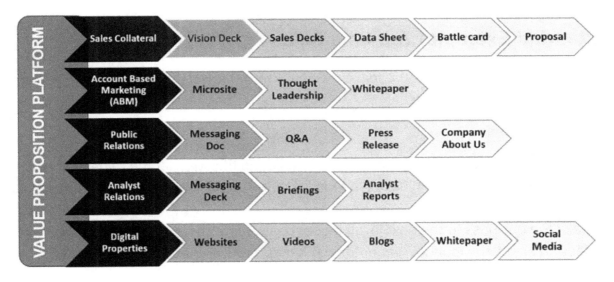

I recommend you make a special outreach to your head of sales and whoever is responsible for sales enablement, if that is a separate function in your organization. In addition to the rollout for your entire company, Sales needs to understand how you will help them build the **Value Proposition Platform** into their sales playbook and their sales training. Plus, you need to discuss how you plan to help them update all current sales materials, both the ones that marketing provides and the ones they have created themselves (some of which they've kept hidden from you). This is a golden opportunity for closer communication between Marketing and Sales if you take advantage of it in a proper way. After all this work, you want to be sure that everyone is telling the same story, on the web, in email, on the telephone, and face-to-face with your buyers.

To maximize the impact in unveiling the new messaging (such as with a redesigned website), be sure to coordinate the date with *all* parties involved, with a "go / no go" status. You don't want mixed-messaging going out into the market which will sink your new approach before you are ready to go all in. So, plan your launch carefully.

Extended Example: Top Line Sales

In the MediaConvo example, the focus was on how we rolled out the value proposition and related messaging to the entire company because that was the most important next step for them.

Top Line Sales, however, is a solopreneur company, and the goals for the value proposition project were very different. In Chapter 4 we listed the goals needed to be accomplished.

1   Take the business to the next level: bigger deals, more revenue predictability, higher fees. In effect, the founder had outgrown her current business.

2   Earn much more money by working more strategically: develop a set of processes or a system that would lead to bigger, longer term, more strategic engagements.

3   Bring in business more predictably: There was a need for more of a social media presence, more visible thought leadership, a compelling value proposition and better messaging.

At the end of this project, Top Line Sales had a compelling value proposition and the basis for a remake of company business offerings, as well as messaging.

Prior to working on the value proposition, the company offerings were as follows:

Top Line Sales provides the following services:

- Strategic Sales Consulting

- One-on-One Sales Coaching

- Sales Management Coaching

- Strategic Sales Training Workshops

- After the new **Value Proposition Platform** was developed, it enabled the organization to revamp the offerings in a very different way.

The TOP Line Account™ System:

- The TOP Line Account™ War Room

- The Strategic Sales Development Workshop

- The Sales Results Coaching System

- The Sales Leadership Excellence Program

- 'Beyond Customer Service' Sales Training

Top Line Sales is now comprised of a system of strategic services, each focused on specific issues and producing specific results. The founder defines it as "The Top Line Account Way," a philosophy, a system, and a methodology. Here is an example of how it begins to be communicated to external audiences as a direct result of all the value proposition work:

The TOP Line Account Way™- Philosophy

- Landing TOP Line Accounts™ has a transformational effect on your business.
- TOP Line Account™ strategy planning pays off with new prospects **and** retention of your largest **and** most important customers.
- Strong leadership following a proven system leads to winning big deals.
- Maneuvering the complex terrain of TOP Line Account™ opportunities is achieved through focus, patience and attention to strategy detail.

The TOP Line Account Way™- System

The engine to turn the entire account team into strategic thinkers and implementers

The TOP Line Account Way™- Methodology

Identify	Assess	Advance	Close	Expand
Spot potential TOP Line Account™ opportunity	Determine whether the opportunity warrants using The TOP Line Account Way™	Move forward with strategic foreknowledge	Facilitate natural outcomes	Restart planning to generate new revenue streams

A comprehensive set of tools supports the system and method. Previously, the company would present a simple list of about 100 tools. Now the tools are organized according to how they support each stage in the method.

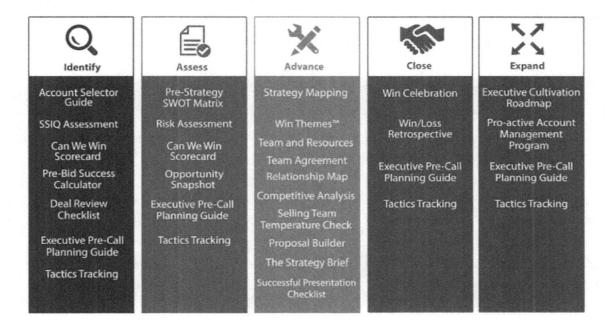

The TOP Line Account Way™- Tools

Identify	Assess	Advance	Close	Expand
Account Selector Guide	Pre-Strategy SWOT Matrix	Strategy Mapping	Win Celebration	Executive Cultivation Roadmap
SSIQ Assessment	Risk Assessment	Win Themes™	Win/Loss Retrospective	Pro-active Account Management Program
Can We Win Scorecard	Can We Win Scorecard	Team and Resources		
Pre-Bid Success Calculator	Opportunity Snapshot	Team Agreement Relationship Map	Executive Pre-Call Planning Guide	Executive Pre-Call Planning Guide
Deal Review Checklist	Executive Pre-Call Planning Guide	Competitive Analysis	Tactics Tracking	Tactics Tracking
		Selling Team Temperature Check		
Executive Pre-Call Planning Guide	Tactics Tracking	Proposal Builder		
		The Strategy Brief		
Tactics Tracking		Successful Presentation Checklist		

Please visit the website at **www.toplinesales.com** to see more of this value proposition in action. Don't be surprised if it has been upgraded since then. A value proposition should be reviewed at least annually to be sure that it still reflects your buyers' perspectives.

Post-script – Lisa Magnuson, founder of Top Line Sales, reports that her **"revenues doubled due to bigger and better engagements from 2013 on."** That revenue impact began one year after she finished the value proposition work.

In summary, a better, clearer, buyer-focused message works. Fact. It sets you apart from competitors who are doing the same old product or service pitch. By putting the buyer's face in the mirror, you have a *decided advantage* in gaining their attention. If the offer makes sense for them, you already have a significant edge in getting on their short list. As the research told us, getting on the short list makes the difference. 96% of our survey respondents told us they end up making a purchase from the vendor that offered relevant value propositions that most aligned with their interests and needs.

VALUE POINTS
Create a version of your value proposition for each distinct audience to which you sell, and for different industries or distinctly different products or services.
Version differences primarily exist in the buyer objective statement and in the value drivers and accompanying quantifications and proof.
Use your value proposition to update your messaging in all your marketing and sales materials, both existing materials and new ones.
Build your value proposition content into your sales enablement materials and training.

11

Value Propositions in Buying Decisions: The Research Study

In 2014, I conducted a survey of 300 B2B buyers to understand how value propositions figure into the decision process of buying teams who are making technology-related investments. I was the lead researcher and research analyst for this research study, which my company, Knowledgence Associates, conducted in partnership with IDG Connect.

Knowledgence® Associates, a consulting firm founded in 1997, focuses on the intersection of Marketing and Sales. Customer engagements concentrate on marketing, sales, and customer program development and execution for business-to-business products and services, with a concentration in the technology, manufacturing, healthcare, professional services, and information industries. We help clients to leverage the marketing and sales knowledge assets that surround their customers, products, competitors, and marketing/sales personnel – designing and executing programs that deliver both sales results and market learning.

www.knowledgence.com, www.ValueProposition.expert

IDG Connect is the demand generation division of International Data Group (IDG), the world's largest technology media company. Established in 2006, it utilizes access to 44 million business decision makers' details to unite technology marketers with relevant targets from 147 countries around the world. Committed to engaging a disparate global IT audience with truly localized messaging, IDG Connect also publishes market specific thought leadership papers on behalf of its clients and produces research for B2B marketers worldwide. www.idgconnect.com/static/about

The data-gathering for the research study was completed in December 2014, and data analysis took place during Q1 2015. However, my experience in working with companies to create their value propositions and use them in their selling process convinces me that these findings are evergreen. Where the respondents predicted how trends would evolve two years into the future, these trends have surpassed their predictions.

My experience also suggests that this research about technology-related purchases can reasonably be extrapolated to other purchase decisions that business-to-business corporate buying teams are called on to make in the course of their executive responsibilities and subject-matter expertise.

In-depth coverage of my research is included in this book, so that you can fully understand what we learned and assess how it fits with your own experience as a buyer and a seller in today's business environment.

My research insights, observations, and words of wisdom have been sprinkled liberally throughout the book where they will be most useful to you; therefore, this chapter simply deals with the data, not the analysis.

Demographics: The Study Respondents

Research was conducted among 300 buying team members from US organizations, using an online survey.

Organizations with 1000-4999 employees formed the majority of the respondents (45%) followed by 10,000 or more employees (32%) and 5000-9999 employees (23%).

The majority of respondents (78%) describe themselves as decision makers; others include consultants (13%) and technical evaluators/recommenders (8%).

The study asked respondents to define their primary area of interest as Business Impact, Technical Impact, or Financial Impact. Technical impact was most important to 47%, followed by Business Impact (34%) and Financial Impact (19%).

Respondents are involved in several technology/service related purchase decisions covering multiple products and services.

Personas of the Respondents

We asked respondents to describe their own style in the decision-making process from among three choices. They chose

1   Collaborator (40%)

2   Challenger (34%)

3   Advocate (26%)

Focus Area in the Buying Process

We identified three "focus areas" as people, processes and outcomes, asking respondents to name their top focus area and their second focus area during their purchase decision process. A significant percentage of respondents placed emphasis on all three focus areas. However, Outcomes is the top focus area for most respondents (Top Focus = 47%, Second Focus = 32%), followed by Processes (Top Focus = 27%, Second Focus = 38%).

Buying Approach

We asked respondents to choose a phrase that best describes their approach when they participate in a purchase decision as part of a buying team.

The choices and percentage of respondents selecting each one are:

- Work as a Team and Weigh all Pros, Cons and Opinions (42%)

- Challenge People's Thoughts, Solutions and Viewpoints (30%)

- Make Things Happen and Take the Best Action (28%)

Research Findings

Buyer Preference for Type of Value Proposition

Vendors can use one of three types of value proposition to communicate their offerings. We asked respondents, how much weight of preference they give to each type today? And what will be the relative weight in two years?

- **Buyer-Focused** (customer needs, challenges, goals)—38% give most weight to this one

- **Features/ Benefit focused** (product or service details only)—35% prefer this one

- **Alternative focused** (vendor vs. competitor offering)—27% prefer this one

The same respondents predict that the relative weight of preference in 2 years will be buyer-focused growing to 42%, while the other two each drop by 2%.

Relevance of the Value Proposition to Buyer Needs

These buyers reported that two-thirds of value propositions offered by vendors are relevant to their needs; however, 93% of respondents feel that value propositions presented by some vendors are better aligned with their needs than those offered by others.

Respondents rated the degree of relevance to range from as low as only 30% to as high as 71% relevant in value propositions for vendors they considered. Almost all respondents (a striking 96%) purchased from the vendor who offered the most relevant value propositions aligned with their interests and needs.

Impact of Value Proposition on the Buying Team's Favorite

Most respondents (85%) said that the vendor that offers the most relevant value propositions is their favorite during the purchase decision process. Most respondents also said that poor alignment of value propositions with buyer needs significantly reduces a vendor's prospects in being recommended for the shortlist (76%) as well reducing their likelihood to buy (68%).

A vendor's failure to demonstrate and explain relevant value propositions aligned with buyer needs and interests decreases the prospects of their solution being:

- recommended for the shortlist (by 35%),

- or purchased (by 47%).

Value Proposition Weaknesses

Respondents noted several weaknesses in value propositions submitted by vendors.

- **Not Relevant to Our Needs** is the most prevalent weakness (chosen by 49% of respondents)

The next most prevalent value proposition weaknesses are:

- Generic Statements (41%)

- No Proof Offered (39%)

- Lack of Quantification (38%)

- Too Promotional (37%)

Other weaknesses identified by respondents include Unclear or Hard to Find, Doesn't Reflect or Connect with Their Brand, No Differentiation, or Too Feature and Function Focused.

Most Important Value Proposition Areas

Most respondents (61%) selected **Relevance to a Specific Need** as the most important area of interest that value propositions can communicate.

The next most important areas of interest are **Impact on Our Organization** (58%) and **Tangible Business Benefits** (54%).

Similarly, given 100 points to assign among important areas of interest that value propositions can communicate, respondents gave more than half of the total to these three areas:

1   **Relevance to a Specific Need** (20 points), **Impact on Our Organization** (18 points), and **Tangible Business Benefits** (15 points) are the most important value proposition areas.

2   Other areas are much less relevant:

   - Identify risks and rewards—11

   - Business justification—11

   - Quantification—10

   - Differentiation from competitors—9

   - Objective 3rd party proof—7

Most Important Value Proposition Areas by Buying Stages

We asked the respondents which value proposition area was most important at each buying stage. Here's how they ranked the top value proposition areas by buying stages:

- **General Education**: Relevance to a Specific Need, Tangible Business Benefits, and Impact on Our Organization

- **Business Case Development**: Impact on Our Organization, Tangible Business Benefits, and Relevance to a Specific Need

- **Implementation Scenarios**: Impact on Our Organization, Address Potential Risks and Rewards, and Tangible Business Benefits

- **Shortlist Creation**: Relevance to a Specific Need, and Impact on Our Organization

- **Final Decisions**: Impact on Our Organization, Relevance to a Specific Need, and Tangible Business Benefits

These responses indicate that buyers respond to value propositions differently at different stages of their buying process, and that sellers need to understand how to craft value propositions that can hold their own at every stage.

Value Level Weight

In their value propositions, vendors may explain different types of value they bring to buyers and the buyers' organization. Three key levels of value that vendors should address are:

- **Ongoing Value**: How they are sustainable and will stay/keep things up and running.

- **Added Value**: How they can enhance your processes, efficiency, effectiveness, insight and performance.

- **New Value**: How they can help you change the competitive rules to enhance success.

We asked respondents how much overall weight they gave to each level of value as they made their purchase decision. They accorded all three levels of value significant importance in the purchase decision process; however, **Ongoing Value** is given the most weight (39 out of 100).

Relative Weight of Organizational Benefits vs. Personal Benefits

Value propositions may identify benefits to the organization as well as benefits specific to the roles and responsibilities of the buyers. The respondents placed higher importance on **Organizational Benefits** (59%) versus **Personal Benefits** (41%) in value propositions. They also predict that Organizational Benefits will continue to assume higher importance over Personal Benefits in the next two years, climbing from 59% to 62% of the total weight of importance.

Impact on Buyer Support of Lack of Personal Benefits in the Value Proposition

Although respondents prefer to see organizational benefits, a significant percentage (62%) said lack of clear personal value to them can decrease the likelihood that they will support a vendor's offer. The degree of influence is high— such lack of a clear statement of personal value decreases the likelihood of their support by 58%.

Relative Weight of Personalization

In order to understand the influence of personal benefits in the buying process more broadly, we posed this question:

> *"Vendors tailor how they engage with you about their offerings in the content they provide and social media conversations they present. Of the ways vendors try to personalize how they engage and educate you (listed below), which one is most important? Least important?"*

This is the list of personalization areas we provided:

- By Product/Service Features

- By My Primary Decision Interest (technical, financial and/or business impact)

- By Areas of Risk, Control and Rewards (practicality, recognition, hassle-free implementation, benefits)

- By My Industry

- By Value Propositions

- By My Decision Role

- By My Organization Size

- By My Job Title

- Respondents give the highest weight of importance to a vendor's ability to personalize conversations and content by **Product/Service Features** (17%). They give significant and marginally distinct importance to all other ways in which vendors can personalize their conversations and content when engaging with them

Areas of Risk, Control and Rewards (14%) and **My Primary Decision Interest** (13%) are the next top areas where respondents desire personalization. **Personalization by Job Title** is least desired, chosen by only 10%, so you can see that the range of most to least importance is very constrained in this question. To reiterate, all the ways that vendors try to personalize engagement and education are important to buyers!

Impact of Failure to Personalize

We asked respondents to determine for each of the engagement factors, if a vendor is unable to tailor their conversation and content, would it negatively impact your interest in their offering and your likelihood to support them as a shortlist candidate?

The most important engagement factors for this response and the percentage of respondents selecting each are:

- Product/Service Features (59%)

- Areas of Risk, Control and Rewards (58%)

- Value Propositions (56%)

- **My Industry** and **My Decision Interest** also received significant responses (48% and 47% respectively)

The actual amount of negative impact related to non- personalization in Product / Service Features has the highest average negative impact on likelihood of being recommended for shortlist (15%) as well as making the shortlist (19%). This is followed by Areas of Risk Control and Rewards (13% and 16% respectively), and finally value propositions (12% and 25% respectively). Of them all, not personalizing the value proposition has the highest negative impact on making the shortlist – a key factor that not handled can potentially disqualify even a strong product or service offering.

Summary

As stated earlier, my summary statements and analysis appear throughout the book. The data is included in this final chapter as supplemental to your understanding, and to satisfy curiosity about any of the research. I will be updating this research within the next year, so please visit my website at **www.valueproposition.expert** for updates and deeper dives in the near future.

ABOUT THE AUTHOR

Lisa D. Dennis
President
Knowledgence Associates
www.ValueProposition.expert
www.knowledgence.com

Lisa Dennis is a global marketing and sales strategist and consultant. She brings over thirty years of marketing and sales experience to her work with business-to-business clients. She founded the consulting firm, Knowledgence Associates, in 1997 with a core focus of helping sales and marketing teams "see the world through their customers' eyes™. She has worked with companies across a broad range of sectors and industries (specialties in high technology, healthcare, insurance, manufacturing, and professional services) including Akamai, Citrix, CSC, Dell, FedEx, HP, Hitachi, IBM, Microsoft, Mutual of Omaha, Tufts Health Plan, Verizon, Wipro and many others.

She has been a guest blogger for TechTarget, Kite Desk, Pipeliner CRM, MassHighTech. com, and a co-author of the book, *360 Degrees of the Customer – Strategies & Tactics for Marketing, Sales and Service.* She has held non-profit board seats for Positive Directions, the YWCA of Cambridge, and The Children's Room. She has a B.A in English with a concentration in Writing from Wheaton College, and an MBA in Marketing from Babson College.